THE LONDON
ENVIRO400

THE LONDON
ENVIRO400

PEN & SWORD TRANSPORT

Matthew Wharmby

Contents

DEDICATION

To Dad

Published in 2016 by Pen & Sword Transport an imprint of Pen & Sword Books Ltd, 47 Church Street, Barnsley, South Yorkshire S70 2AS

Copyright © Matthew Wharmby 2016

ISBN 978 1 47386 231 9

The right of Matthew Wharmby to be identified as the Author of this Work has been asserted by him in accordance with the Copyright, Designs and Patents Act 1988.
A CIP catalogue record for this book is available from the British Library

Typeset by Matthew Wharmby

Printed and bound by Replika Press Pvt. Ltd., India

Pen & Sword Books Ltd incorporates the imprints of Pen & Sword Archaeology, Atlas, Aviation, Battleground, Discovery, Family History, History, Maritime, Military, Naval, Politics, Railways, Select, Transport, True Crime, and Fiction, Frontline Books, Leo Cooper, Praetorian Press, Seaforth Publishing and Wharncliffe.

For a complete list of Pen & Sword titles please contact

PEN & SWORD BOOKS LIMITED
47 Church Street, Barnsley, South Yorkshire, S70 2AS, England

E-mail: enquiries@pen-and-sword.co.uk

Website: www.pen-and-sword.co.uk

Foreword

L ikeable and versatile within the limits of the DDA-imposed low-floor configuration and TfL's own specifications, the Alexander Dennis Enviro400 has settled in as the main second-generation low-floor double-deck London bus, numbering 1,553 units with eighteen contracted operators. Although all must now be in a livery of all-over red, variety is offered by the myriad of advertising liveries as well as the constant flux in fleetnames and fleetnumbers. Technological advancement has also been evident, confidence in battery-hybrid developments ensuring orders in quantities that would eventually surpass those of diesel-engined vehicles.

This book covers the original Enviro400 (and its E40D and E40H developments) to the beginning of March 2016, and incorporates the introduction of its pair of successors, the MMC (Major Model Change) and City, which are sure to grow in numbers sufficient to merit books of their own in the future.

Matthew Wharmby
Walton-on-Thames, March 2016

Below: **The newest Enviro400s at the time of writing are the thirty diesel examples delivered to Arriva Kent Thameside for the 229 and 492 out of Dartford from 23 January 2016, and due to the fact that this operation was to be subsumed within Arriva London North, delivered with traditional class codes. This is T 308 (LK65 ENW), seen at Bexleyheath on 18 February.**
Matthew Wharmby

Go-Ahead London

E 1-284, EH 1-39

Never particularly taken with the Dennis Trident, the Go-Ahead Group only ever owned fifty of them by comparison with some other companies which had hundreds. All Plaxton President-bodied, the PDL class was solely allocated to Stockwell, PDLs 1-13 being new in 2000, PDLs 14-27 in 2002 and PDLs 28-50 in 2003. None survived the seven years that is the maximum term of a single contract and all were gone by 2010. Yet it was to prove a major customer for the Enviro400, which, after all, is based on an only subtly modified Trident chassis. In September 2005, as prototypes were being readied for display on the circuit of commercial motor shows, Go-Ahead placed its first order for fifteen, to fulfil the takeover of the 196 from 6 May 2006. Although it had been used to Volvo B7TLs for its first-generation low-floor double-deck stock and had taken 464 of them (419 PVLs and 45 AVLs) in five years, a noise problem had manifested itself sufficient for a ban to be imposed by TfL on their purchase until this could be remedied, thus giving competitors an opportunity that could become a permanent fixture if they were liked enough. Even before the 196's Es had arrived, 24 more

Left: **The Enviro400's rear was perhaps a little fussy, with its mobile phone-shaped rear window, but it showed a little more imagination when faced with the fact that a low-floor design made the back and sides of a bus not match on height levels. The three vents are for the exit of used air from the air-blowing system fitted above the staircase. This shot is of Stockwell's E 4 (SN06 BNE) at Vauxhall on 13 May 2006.** *Matthew Wharmby*

were ordered in February 2006 to supply the 37, which had been retained on tender and was operating at the moment from Peckham with AVLs. It was at this point that the class code E was selected; simple and to the point, reflecting the integral nature of the bus that Alexander Dennis was keen to promote (and in spite of the fact that the manufacturer's plates inside the doorway still read (and ten years on, still do read!) DENNIS TRIDENT 2.

To H41/26D layout on a 10.1m chassis, the improved capacity downstairs was courtesy of the seats over the front wheelarches.

The Es were also the first Euro 4-specification buses in London, powered by Cummins ISB4e engines cleaned by SCR technology (AdBlue). This was made much of by TfL, which displayed Es 6-8 and 11 at Covent Garden on 27 April. During that month E 1 made a visit to Dublin Bus, and on 6 May the class made its service debut. Inside was a refreshed look with new moquette to a bluer pattern without the displaced pattern used previously; handrails remained yellow, sidewalls blue and the floor dark blue with sparkles.

Left: **On 9 December 2006, a date when attention was otherwise focused on the Routemasters to be found in the area commemorating the first anniversary of the withdrawal of the type from public service, E 1 (SN06 BNA) passes through Brixton.** *Matthew Wharmby*

Left: **Peckham's contingent of Es for the 37 followed on the heels of the 196's batch, replacing AVLs. Two years later E 21 (LX06 EZR) is still in original condition as it reposes at the 37's latter-day Putney Heath, Green Man stand on 5 May 2008.** *Matthew Wharmby*

Middle: **E 28 (LX06 EZC) by night as this 37 pauses at East Putney station on 7 October 2006.** *Matthew Wharmby*

Delivery of the second batch commenced in the third week of May, the new Es being stored before service entry at Mandela Way or Peckham, but despite the new contract on the 37 taking effect from 3 June, they entered service only in dribs and drabs, the first four venturing out on 7 June. This order included two (Es 38 and 39) to top up the 87 upon its rather arbitrary renumbering from 77A the same day, although Es could soon be seen on all of Stockwell's services, the 88 and 133 being early sightings, and Es even managed to get out twice on the 77A before its withdrawal. Es 38 and 39 were delivered by 4 July, although they carried numberplates already allocated to LDPs and had to be corrected first. The 37, while receiving a slight re-routeing in East Dulwich that took it away from the station, was also intended to be re-routed from its historic Putney stand to terminate at Putney Heath, where a significantly enlarged stand had been carved out opposite the Green Man, but this wasn't implemented until 2 September. Peckham soon let its new buses wander to the 63 and 363, PVLs (and AVLs while still based) making return appearances as fit. The N36 at night also saw Es. During July Stockwell Es racked up visits to the 11 and 345, but it was not until 2007 that they had a try on the 333 and the 170 was restricted to Darts, ruling that one out.

In August 2006 an order was placed for 17 more Es to fulfil the requirement for the 486, retained on tender by London Central's Bexleyheath and representing an upgrade from the current DAF SB220LC single-deckers (MDs). The contract date was 24 February 2007. It was also commonplace by now to include a double-decker as a schools component to a single-deck order, and a single further E was added to ongoing deliveries in November so as to be ready to replace the 200's PVL currently employed on this role in the New Year.

Left: **Seen at Clapham Common on 13 February 2011, Peckham's E 21 (LX06 EZR) still looks in good shape for five years' worth of service.** *Matthew Wharmby*

Right and middle: **The 486 had begun as a faintly gimmicky pair of routes designed to take visitors from the two major railheads to the Millennium Dome. The Greenwich leg withered on the vine, but the Charlton one had promise and it was this that was revamped into the 486 and projected ever further southeastwards, first to Welling and then even further to Bexleyheath, which thus had three direct links to North Greenwich. On 3 March 2007 E 45 (LX56 ETL) is seen in deepest Charlton, and later in the day it is captured on its way back past the new Sainsbury's at Bugsby's Way.** *Both: Matthew Wharmby*

January 2007 saw the first of Bexleyheath's intended allocation arrive; familiarisation with the chassis had already been achieved through the loan of Stockwell's E 10 on 15 December. E 40 was delivered on 19 January and was put to work training drivers on the 22nd; E 41 arrived on the 24th. Es 41 and 43 were loaned to London General's Commercial Services department at Merton on 1 February for a rail replacement at short notice, marking the class's debut on this type of work, and later in the month two Es got as far as Chichester. Service entry of E 40-56 proceeded as planned, all seventeen taking over the 486 from its MDs and VWL 1 a day early on 23 February, after the appearance of a single example the day before that. The three gas-powered DAFs had already been stood down and that type of fuel not explored again. While contracted to run the 486, Bexleyheath's Es were blinded for the garage's other routes and soon started wandering to the 51, 89, 229, 401 and 422. From this batch, opening emergency-exit upper-deck rear windows were specified rather than the fixed glass units with hammer provided.

Left: **On 3 March 2007 Bexleyheath's E 56 (LX56 EUD) sets off from Charlton station for the long slog uphill that would take the 486 beyond the limited objectives realised for it and towards where people that needed it lived; links to the Tube were felt tenuous in south-east London despite there being plenty of railways to take workers to central London.** *Matthew Wharmby*

Four more Es were ordered in February 2007 for unspecified service increases, which in March was revealed to be to the 213 at Sutton; in the interests of standardisation (always a problem when ordering small numbers of new chassis) the intent to add an E to the 200 was superseded and E 57 was allocated to Stockwell when it arrived. In spite of this broadly sensible but slightly unfair policy which had led to more than a few routes London-wide being done out of their intended new buses, Es 58-61 did indeed enter service at Sutton in the third week of June; the 213 had gained its PVR boost on 31 March. Plans to put the Es into Stockwell to release four WVLs to Putney for their own needs on the 85 thus fell through, and the Sutton Es remained the only examples of their type there, naturally soon wandering to the 93, 151 and 154 in lieu of an EVL and even displacing single-decks at times on the 80, 163 and 164.

London General was boosted during the spring with the announcement of the award of the 24 from Metroline for a November takeup. Uniquely completely unchanged since 1912, the 24 was actually harder to run than it looked, and no contractor since Grey-Green would last more than a single term. An order was placed for 32 more Es, which would take operation of the route south of the river for the first time by being based at Stockwell. General increases to all routes were now the order of the day, reflecting London's ever-increasing population and their needs, and in July six more Es were ordered, to add to the 36's PVR from February 2008. New Cross was another garage not to have had experience with the class before (even in its Trident form), but mixed operation was no longer a taboo. Plans had been kicked around to put the six Es into Peckham and release PVLs, but direct operation was preferred again.

E 1 and 2 enjoyed a day out to the races on 2 June 2007 with their visit to the traditional Derby Day 406F route from Morden station, while E 57 was out on the Wimbledon tennis service later that month.

The transfer of the 24 from Metroline to London General on 10 November exchanged one set of Enviro400s (the Holloway TEs that had come in at the beginning of 2006) for another (Stockwell's new E 62-93). The 133 discounted itself from possible E operation with its move to Mandela Way to clear space, but more Es at Stockwell meant more appearances on routes not intended

for them. Es 74-81 were delayed in delivery, requiring older Es to fill in on the 24 as priority; they were released for the duration by additional PVLs loaned from New Cross to join incumbent WVLs on the 196. A seating capacity reduction was evident, this batch being H39/25D with a little more legroom upstairs and a single seat opposite the exit door downstairs.

On 11 February Stockwell's E 2 was driven too far to the left-hand side of the road underneath the bridge in Prince of Wales Road while on diversion due to a major fire at Camden Market two days earlier and was deroofed under the protruding arch. It was repaired and back in service by 19 June.

Es 94-99 were delivered in April and allocated to New Cross for the 36's upcount that had already gone ahead on 9 February using existing PVLs; the first appearance on the 36 was by E 94 on 10 April, but for the moment the sextet stayed put on their assigned route without wandering. Obliquely related was the use of the Enviro400 body design on three Volvo B9TLs delivered to London General in September and allocated to the 85 as the VE class; while no more were ordered, Go-Ahead began ordering Volvo chassis in bulk again, adding new Wright-bodied B9TLs to the WVL class and thus

holding off on more E purchases for the time being, though the purchase of WVLs and Es simultaneously would hark back to the old dual-sourcing purchasing patterns employed by London Transport so as to head off any possible delivery delays. You could even call it triple-sourcing, given that the order for 54 double-deckers for the Sutton contracts that year materialised as 'Tridents' with Optare Olympus bodywork (DOE 1-54); a second batch of unique buses for Sutton to follow its EVLs.

iBus equipment was fitted to Go-Ahead Group buses during 2008, London Central's Peckham and Bexleyheath preceding Stockwell and Sutton where E operators were concerned. A wild period of loans during this process saw Metroline TPLs used at Stockwell, followed by TNs from First; both were broadly identical to the garage's indigenous PDLs other than by coding and interior.

Despite the takeover of Sutton by the DOE class from December 2007, Es 58-61 stayed put and indeed didn't restrict themselves to the 213 any longer; on the 6th the 51 was removed from the roster of Bexleyheath routes likely to see E appearances via its loss to Selkent, and the PDL class at Stockwell started to be stood down.

Towards the end of 2008 the hybrid version of the Enviro400 was developed, known as the Enviro400H, and tentative orders were placed for small batches. Go-Ahead ordered five as EH 1-5 to be run alongside the Es on the 24, while competing chassis from both Wrights (WHD 1) and Volvo (WHV 1) were taken in single numbers at the same time. EH 1 had a further seating reduction to 62 (H37/25D) due to the presence of the battery packs at the rear of the upper deck. Type training was carried out late in January and EH 1 entered service on the 24 on 4 February. EHs 3 and 4 followed on the 17th, taking up service on the 196, and EHs 2 and 5 rounded out the quintet. The 196 tended to take priority at first because it stopped outside Stockwell garage for immediate attention if needed, but as the vehicles settled in, increasing use was made of them on the 24. On 31 March the EHs were officially transferred to the 24.

Awarded to and retained by London General in September 2008, the 345 and its night counterpart needed new buses, and 2009 was started off with a healthy order for 29 more Es to be delivered to accompany contract assumption on 2 May. They comprised Es 100-128 and were allocated to Stockwell over June, July and into August, quickly becoming mixed with their older counterparts which in turn made their way

Middle and right: **Tremendously busy ever since its separation fron the 45 (as 45A), today's 345 quickly threw off its Dart SLFs for WVLs and PVLs, but in 2009 it was refreshed for a new contract with 29 new Es. Both sighted on 13 February 2011 at Clapham Common, the overcast allowing clear shots of either side of the road without shadows, Es 107 (LX09 FAM) and 128 (LX09 FCE) have running lights.** *Matthew Wharmby*

Above: **An example of an E wandering off its assigned route is Sutton's E 58 (LX07 BYC), which on 14 November 2009 finds itself in Wimbledon as a 93. The quartet could also be put out on the 151 and 154 if Sutton had a mind to it.**
Matthew Wharmby

stocked with refurbished PVLs in place of the outgoing EVLs, could still see the four Es as well as DOEs from Sutton's other three double-deck services. The rest of 2009 was quiet as the Group concentrated on buying Volvo B9TLs in bulk; not unlike the old days of M and T segregation, the WVL variety of B9s and Es seemed to be apportioned in the same geographical manner between Londons Central and General! The Docklands Buses and Blue Triangle operations picked up across the river, meanwhile, were about to take WVLs. At New Cross an E was sighted away from the 36 for the first time when E 94 popped up on the 171 on 12 October. During November Stockwell's E 6 was loaned to Peckham, having to turn out with makeshift blinds, and it was not out of the question for Peckham's new WVLs for the 63 to turn out on the 37, together with the refurbished PVLs allocated to the 363 at the same time. The new WVLs allocated to the 21 at New Cross were also apt to visit the 36. Following on from the EH's trip to Brighton, E 35 was used there on 21-23 July, WVL 310 setting out there a week later for comparison. The company subsequently chose the latter chassis, and in some strength.

In May the 88's award was announced as a retention by London General with a mix of existing and new buses, and in the same month the 118 was also retained. A combined order for 22 more Es was thus placed in August, which would bring numbers up to E 150 and give Merton its first examples of the type (although DOE 54 had been based there alone since being tacked on to the end of the order for that class as the double-deck enhancement). In September the 337 was won back from Arriva presenting London and the 196 retained with the existing buses, thus prolonging the Es' careers for at least five more years and with the promise of more, meaning that after a very slow 2009 and 2010 things would be picking up for the E class. New workings for 2010 included a lone Sutton E on the 164 and a New Cross one on the 321.

The year was thus rounded out with the delivery in late November of Es 129-137 for the 'new bus' component of the 88; first sightings were on the 27th, with the balance for the 118 awaited in 2011. This time the upper-deck capacity was back to the original specification, seating 41 to 26 downstairs.

2011 was set to be a bumper year; in December not only was the 337's order firmed up as twelve Es, but forty-two more were added, thought at this point to be for the

to the 345 as fit. The new buses seated 65 (H39/26D) and weighed in at 11520kg, which although a slight improvement on the 11710kg of the first 99 Es (and definitely over the hefty 12090kg of the EHs) hardly represented an improvement in capacity over kerb weight; they seated two fewer than a short Routemaster, weighed over three tons more and were unlikely ever to approach even a third of that class's longevity! Even so, they were the way of the future, with prices likely to be coming down as soon as they proved their mettle, and between 12 and 15 August Brighton & Hove took EH 2 on loan.

On 4 July the 213 at Sutton gained a night counterpart to allow the withdrawal of the N213; the route, while now officially

double-decking of the 12 after seven years of artics. Merton's Es were delivered starting on 18 December and four turned out on the 118 on the 30th in advance of the 5 February 2011 contract-renewal date, almost immediately spreading their net to the 44, 77, 155 and 280 and, by May, the Sunday allocation on the 22. At the same time Bexleyheath's PVL fleet was under replacement by WVLs, which occasionally turned up on the 486 in lieu of an E, but the rest of Merton's new Es were actually held back at Belvedere and not put

into service on the 118 until 10-13 February. New Cross's Es had been kept rigidly to the 36 since delivery, but from this year were seen wandering more often to the 21 and 172.

Even as new Es were on the production lines at Falkirk, the existing ones were now coming due for refurbishment, the effective modern replacement for the Aldenham overhaul by which after five (or seven) years of a contract that had been renewed with the existing operator, the buses were refreshed mechanically and internally for the duration

Above: **It's still hard to imagine the 88 veering off to the north once it reaches Oxford Circus rather than continuing west to Notting Hill and Acton Green, but the route has recovered somewhat from the mad period of slashing during the 1980s and 1990s that meant it still terminates no further south than Clapham Common. A new contract fell due in 2011 and was provisioned at least partially with new Es, one of which is E 134 (SN60 BZF), seen at Oxford Circus on 1 July 2012.**
Matthew Wharmby

Left: **Another curious modern anomaly is the 118 operated from Merton, well off route, rather than the historic Brixton or Streatham, but that's where tendering landed it in 2000 and where it's been ever since. A new contract term for London General spawned an order for thirteen Enviro400s, bringing the E class to Merton for the first time. On 30 July 2011, E 141 (SN60 BZD) heads south from Brixton – again a modern affectation, the route until 1990 having terminated at Clapham Common.**
Matthew Wharmby

Right: **Stockwell's E 10 (SN06 BNU) operates a 196 through Brixton on 11 July 2011; all that distinguishes its refurbishment that year, other than the generally good presentation, is the new Go-Ahead logo on front and sides replacing the old London General logo.**
Matthew Wharmby

Right: **The 24 and 196 saw a lot more mixing of E batches at Stockwell than did the 88 and 345 at first, but the 345 was eventually reallocated away and the 196 lost. Demonstrating as much variety as is possible with an otherwise standardised fleet is E 1 (SN06 BNA) in Camden on 29 August 2011.**
Matthew Wharmby

of another five-to-seven-year contract term. Stockwell's Es 1-15 from the 196's contract (renewed with effect from 7 May 2011) were the first to go to Hants & Dorset Trim from March, managing to be outshopped in a new coat of the existing London General livery with black window surrounds and grey skirt which was otherwise declared outlaw. They now bore the latest Go-Ahead logos which relegated the subsidiary company to a smaller font underneath, and a little later, filled white roundels with 'BUSES' across the bar began appearing on bus sides. Coincident with the rather extreme expedient of removing buses' tip-up seats in the wheelchair area lest opportunists sue for injuries real or manufactured, the buses were downseated from H41/26D to H41/24D.

A slew of orders placed in April covered the impending conversions of the 12, 436 and 453 from artic to double-deck, and for the first time there was money to buy hybrids in bulk, allotted by the Green Fund budget over a particular year. The Enviro400H component constituted 15 EHs to the 41 diesel-engined Es, and there were 16 new WHVs to join 33 WVLs in the best dual-sourcing tradition. After a lull it was decided to allocate the Es to the 453, which would continue to operate out of London General's Mandela Way garage following a decision not to reallocate it to New Cross, while the Volvos would go to the 12 at Peckham. For the 436, 41 more Es and 15 EHs would bring stock numbers to E 245 and EH 20 respectively. The 89 had also been retained in March with a new vehicle

component required for later in the year, and despite the 89 and 229 having been renewed with WVLs, twenty of the Es would be going to Bexleyheath.

E 151-162 were delivered in May and put into service on the 28th as per contract. Unusually for Stockwell Es, this batch has kept very much to its assigned route, wanderings elsewhere being comparatively rare, and nor have earlier Es made much of a venture to the 337 in return, it tending to be WVLs that fill in.

The autumn of the artics was now at hand; the 436 and 453 had both been scheduled to lose their MALs on 19 November, but the conversion of the 453 was brought forward to 24 September in the expectation that all of the new Es would have been delivered. Like the 337's batch, all had Edinburgh registrations once again now that registering buses had been left to the manufacturers, and all were most unfortunately in all-over red by TfL decree, exposing the clumsier of the lines of the design and looking simply uninteresting. There was one last bus in London General livery, however; E 173 was a holdover from when the order for the 337 had been reduced from 13 to 12 to accommodate the PVR's reduction from 12 to 11 buses; it was added to the current batch and deployed to Mandela

Right: Go-Ahead's twin-pronged onslaught against the artic scourge was carried out at the end of 2011 so that the Mayor could count one of his promises fulfilled before the next election. First out were the 453's MALs, replaced by new Es (or at least as soon as the full complement could displace the stand-in PVLs!), and here at Trafalgar Square on 16 October is Mandela Way's E 181 (SN61 BHU), showing the subtle alterations to the lighting and bumper design. *Matthew Wharmby*

Right: After spirited resistance against the drive to all-over red livery, London General finally succumbed late in 2011 with its batch of Es for the 453; all except one. This had been kept back after the order for the 337 had been reduced by one and then added to the group's next order, fitting into the middle of it as E 173 (SN61 BGE). When captured on 8 March 2013 it is making use of the right-turn lane reinstituted for buses needing to reach Whitehall from the south without having to circumnavigate Parliament Square. *Matthew Wharmby*

Right: There had been two sites on Mandela Way, one of them the responsibility of East Thames Buses, but when this company was sold by TfL to Go-Ahead, the other premises was activated as an operational garage and the 453 was taken up from there when it had been won with artics. Now the 453 was E-operated, and spread its new buses with regularity to the 1, on which E 196 (SN61 BJZ) is seen on 1 April 2014 between St George's Circus and the Elephant. *Matthew Wharmby*

Way to form the batch E 163-201. Es 202-204 were allocated to Bexleyheath to herald its own permanent allocation after the 436 was done.

As 24 September loomed, London General realised that it had been too confident bringing the 453's double-decking forward, as they were still short a dozen Es, but juggled some of the incoming WVLs intended for the 12 eight weeks later by putting them on the 45 to release sixteen PVLs to join what Es had made it to Mandela Way for the 453. This garage had also taken over the responsibility of the 1 after its acquisition with the rest of the former East Thames Buses operations, and Es quickly turned out on that too. Its contract renewal date actually took place on 19 November, separate to the type change, and it was on this date that the 436 assumed its new Enviro400 and Enviro400H fleet – or, to be correct, chassis designations E40D and E40H respectively to signify design changes under European legislation. Frontally, the fascia was subtly altered, the bumpers gaining a 'wing' effect and the light panels given a hollow into which it was hoped operators would have added a bank of LED marker lights (none in London ever did, as it turned out, and Stagecoach insisted on keeping the original headlight clusters for

Middle and right: **The conversion of the 436 put an end to bendy buses at Go-Ahead, and this route was given a spot of variety through a third of the new allocation being hybrids. Physically, there are almost no differences between fellow New Cross E 215 (SN61 DDO), seen at Vauxhall on 1 June 2013, and EH 7 (SN61 BLK), approaching Vauxhall on a sunny 24 February 2014 , so a (somewhat too) discreet leaf emblem has had to be added to the E40H, lest the wrong fuel be put in.** *Both: Matthew Wharmby*

Right: **Bexleyheath's intake for the 89 comprised Es 229-245, and sure enough, they could soon be seen on everything else. Here at the Market Place on 4 August 2012 is E 242 (YX61 DPU).** *Matthew Wharmby*

Below: **The 89 had settled back at Bexleyheath after a long spell of exclusively New Cross operation. After an uninspiring run westward, the route's terrain became more interesting with the steep climb over Shooters Hill and the home stretch crossed ever-idyllic Blackheath, which is what E 243 (YX61 DPV) is doing when captured from the upper deck of another oncoming 89 on 4 August 2012.** *Matthew Wharmby*

every subsequent order!). All of Mandela Way's Es were in place by 26 October and Bexleyheath took Es 202-204 plus Es 205-207 to release WVLs to Camberwell to complete the 12; it was then the turn of New Cross's 436, which was allocated Es 208-228 and EHs 6-20 on 19 November. All of Go-Ahead's artics were now gone, and another lull would ensue for E orders after the splurge of 2011. The final members of this batch, Es 229-245, were delivered during January 2012 and entered service at Bexleyheath en masse on the 28th; another difference ensued in that they were built at Scarborough, the former Plaxton factory sold but subsequently re-absorbed into Alexander Dennis. The Beverley registrations (YX61...) were the giveaway here.

In March 2012 15 Es were ordered for the 280, retained on tender by London General; it was envisaged that they would be used on Olympics work once delivered in June and then moved to Merton in September. On 31 March a sweeping set of tendering victories brought the 19 and 249 to London General, but to free space at Stockwell for the former, the 345 was reallocated to Camberwell with its E batch (E 100-128). Believe it or not, these were the first transfers of the E class in its history, and E 61 was simultaneously transferred from Sutton to Peckham, leaving just three Es helping out the DOEs and PVLs there. Camberwell's new intake could soon be sighted on the X68.

Also on 31 March, the Group's Enviro400 complement increased by 24 when the

Left: **One London-spec Enviro400 is much like the next, other than inside. This bus was new to First Capital as DN 33539 but was accepted into London General on 31 March 2012 as EH 13 (SN58 CFD), and with a new logo applied on the front at least, is seen leaving Turnpike Lane on 11 August 2012.** *Matthew Wharmby*

operations of First Capital's Northumberland Park garage were acquired as part of a phased sell-off of First's London holdings. DNs 33527-33543 and 33520-33526 thus became EN 1-24 and continued to operate the 191 and 231 though now with London General legal lettering. Visits to the 67, 357 and 476 were also within their remit. It was to Northumberland Park that the first of this year's new Es were delivered in June before fanning out to operate variously on the Hampton Court Flower Show, the Wimbledon tennis service and the link to and from the Farnborough air show. 2012 saw the first all-over ads reach Es, E 48 touting the Samsung Galaxy S2 and Es 40, 56, 58 and 69 Visa, all five at Bexleyheath. Es 38 and 39 were transferred there from Stockwell in July to release some PVLs over the river to Docklands Buses for Olympics enhancements. The Games proved successful and popular and were followed soon after by the Paralympics at the same venues. E 246-260, which had not received any fleetnames to comply with Olympics rules over commercial competition, promptly redeployed to Bexleyheath and took over the 132 on 28 August, assisted by Es 38, 39 and now 57 on loan from Stockwell. This ad-hoc double-decking obliged questions to be asked about whether this route, and the 129 over much the same roads, should convert full-time. The simultaneous retention on tender of Northumberland Park's 231 and the longer-established 44, 77 and 87 promised a component of new buses alongside existing ones with Es (or ENs) sure to play a part. E 210 received a Vodafone advert in July and Es 42, 45, 54, 138, 139, 141, 217 and 218 followed suit in August.

Middle and left: **The all-over advert craze came comparatively late to the Enviro400, but was adopted with a vengeance during Olympics year 2012. These two Bexleyheath vehicles were ideally placed to spread sponsors' messages to the masses come to watch the Games; E 48 (LX56 ETT) at Bexleyheath on 4 August for Samsung and E 54 (LX56 EUB) on 8 September for Vodafone, also at Bexleyheath.** *Both: Matthew Wharmby*

Left: **Wandering off the 37 to the 63 on 24 February 2013 is Peckham's E 19 (LX06 EZO). Es could also be seen on the 363, with PVLs and WVLs coming onto the 37 in return.**
Matthew Wharmby

Camberwell's recently-received Es received blinds for the whole garage's double-deck runout in August, allowing theoretical appearances on the 12, 42, 45, 68, X68, 185 and 468, and indeed two were allocated to the 12 for fuel comparison trials with the WVLs and WHVs from 3 September; these were Es 100 and 101. The X68 was an early adopter, but E 176 on 28 August was a loan from Mandela Way.

After their spell on the 132, Es 246-260 transferred between 10-12 September to New Cross, releasing half of the the 36's incumbent PVLs to Merton so that they could form the 'existing' allocation on the 44 and 77 as per the tender; the 280 wouldn't end up getting new buses at all, or at least not of its own. The New Cross intake was less shy than the 08-reg batch had been about drifting to the 21, 171 and 321. Es 38 and 57 returned to Stockwell but E 39 remained at Bexleyheath. In October fifteen more Es were ordered so that the 36 could be completed and the remaining PVLs could head off to Merton and refurbishment, thereby displacing the oldest remaining PVLs which by now were in a really rough state! The balance of Merton's requirements would be filled by Es coming from the 24 when it was lost on 10 November after a single five-year term, but already vehicles from that batch were beginning to move away when E 67 was transferred to Bexleyheath in October. E 48 lost its all-over ad that month.

Bus & Coach held at the NEC on 6 November saw Go-Ahead's announcement of an order for five more E40Ds alongside 18 more E40Hs; the latter were theoretically for the 87, which alone among the Merton and Stockwell tenders waiting to take effect from 1 June 2013 had a 'new bus' component. Four of the Es were to assist the PVL, WVL and older E mix on the 77 at Merton and the fifth was to form the 'new bus' requirement for the 231 at Northumberland Park from 8 June 2013. The 24 was duly lost to Metroline on 10 November and its Es began moving into Merton, displacing X-reg PVLs to Bexleyheath to formally double-deck the 132 after its successful spell as such during

Below: **The loss of the 24 after one term, and not even with a two-year extension at that, meant that homes had to be found for the first five EHs as well as the normal Es. For the moment they stayed put at Stockwell, but appeared most often on the 333, like EH 3 (LX58 DDL) is doing at Streatham, St Leonard's Church, on 14 April 2013.**
Matthew Wharmby

the summer. EHs 1-5 remained at Stockwell ostensibly for the 87 but could only turn out on the 196 and 333 for the moment until new blinds were manufactured; this was where about half of the ex-24 Es remained until they were needed at Merton. Refurbishment of the E 94-98 batch of New Cross Es was carried out at the end of 2012, the work being done at Hants & Dorset in Eastleigh (losing a seat in the process to render them H39/24D), and a similar physical change saw six Es take on all-over ads for Apple's latest iPod in November; these were Es 44, 51, 147, 211, 221 and 228, all but E 147 Bexleyheath-based. Es 94-98 of course came back in all-over red, and so did the iPod ads over the turn of the year.

2013 began with loans to Camberwell for the X68 in the form of Stockwell E 66 and 69, with debut appearances of an E on the 42 and an EH on the 36 during January. Double-deck operation of the 129 was ramped up from 15 January with the appearance in strength of Es from the 36's batch (E 261-275) which were delivered towards the end of the month and completed the ouster of its 54-reg PVLs. The 57-reg Es now took their turn for refurbishment including red repaint, all being done by July 2013 at Hants & Dorset and similarly also being downseated to H39/24D.

From time to time mistakes are made matching the chassis number on the V5 document to its registration, and such was the case when four of the most recent New Cross batch were noticed not to be what they seemed; thus Es 247-250 had their registrations swapped, E 247 taking the mark from E 250 and the other three 'stepping back' one alphabetically. E 240 was absent over the New Year, having suffered an accident on 1 December and not being repaired until March. E 231 had a vehicle proximity system fitted by a company in Lewes and was sighted there on 19 March.

Top, Middle and Left: **Three New Cross Es, one from each batch. E 96 (LX08 EBV) at Harrow Road on 26 August 2003 exemplifies the 2008 batch of five in all-red refurbished form, E 259 (YX12 FPU) at Peckham on 14 April 2003 the batch originally intended for Merton's route 280 but which ended up on the 36, and E 274 (SN62 DLZ) at Waterloo on 27 January 2014 one of the 36's proper batch, but showing its capability of being used on the 171, otherwise the province of WVLs.**
Matthew Wharmby

Left: **Stockwell's loss was Merton's gain as most of the 24's displaced Es went onto the 44 and 77 as the 'existing' component of those important routes' latest contracts. E 86 (LX57 CKV) is calling at Tooting Broadway on 24 February 2013, before repaint out of its London General livery.** *Matthew Wharmby*

Left: **How bare and glum the Es looked after repaint, wasting all the advantages of their interior refurbishment, offering no distinction from any other London bus company and thereby questioning the whole point of having privatised them in the first place. The 118 was already E operated but had its own batch; E 76 (LX57 CKE), seen at Brixton garage on 23 July 2013, is an incomer.** *Matthew Wharmby*

Left: **As for the 118's batch of Es, here is one of them straying onto the 155 on 16 June 2013; E 142 (SN60 BZP) has come to the end of its route 155 journey from the Elephant to Tooting Broadway and is about to turn for St George's Hospital hospital grounds. A spot where the black masking has been missed before re-applying the fleetnumber (presumably after a mishap) does not detract from the clean condition of the bus, set off to its best by the perfect angle of sunlight to take a shot at that time of day.** *Matthew Wharmby*

Of the five E40Ds in this year's order, E 276-279 were intended for Merton and E 280 for Northumberland Park, but when they arrived in June it was E 276 that had been fitted at the factory with Northumberland Park blinds, so rather than go through the fuss of taking the blinds out (a much more complicated task than hitherto, what with powerblinds and iBus to consider), this split was retained and E 276 became the 231's reinforcement starting on 31 May. Es 277-279 entered service at Merton on 18 May and E 280 two days after. All five reverted to Edinburgh plates due to having been constructed at Falkirk. However, a change in plan for the accompanying EHs took them off the 87 (which they had already started appearing on) and reallocated them to the 88 under TfL instructions in accordance with their latest imperative to improve recorded air quality on certain central London corridors; in the same manner that the 22 had to cede its new WHVs to the 74, the 87 now had to make do with the dregs of Stockwell's fleet.

Following on from the sale of Northumberland Park to Go-Ahead the previous year, First now liquidated its entire London portfolio, dividing it on 22 June between Tower Transit (a new offshoot of Australian-owned Transit Holdings), Metroline and Stagecoach. Part of Dagenham depot's routes and their vehicles passed to Go-Ahead under Blue Triangle responsibility, bringing to Rainham three Enviro400s, route 498-based DNs 33501, 33502 and 33505 which were appended to the EN class as ENs 25-27.

In June E 216 gained an all-over ad for *Despicable Me 2* for a month, with E 219 gaining one for Lycamobile. The Vodafone ads reverted to red during July and August. Refurbishment work commenced on an earlier batch of Es during the summer, E 23 going to Hants & Dorset as the vanguard of the 37's batch (to accompany its retention on tender with a new contract from 1 June). The 486's batch would find themselves in the queue for similar treatment due to that route's also having been retained but in this

Above: **Three more Enviro400s accrued to the Go-Ahead Group with the takeover of First's outer operations, but the inheritors, Blue Triangle, had presided over a shocking plummet in standards since its days as Roger Wright's repository of classic buses. To that end, the First Capital fleetnumber on EH 25 (LK57 EJN) is still there as this bus works through Romford on 7 July 2013.** *Matthew Wharmby*

Left: **Another all-over ad was for the Universal animated film *Despicable Me 2*; here is New Cross's E 216 (SN61 DDU) at Marble Arch on 16 June 2013. It is a shame that the effect of the ads is watered down to near-anonymity by TfL's insistence that the front be in fleet colours, meaning that people waiting for the bus will never see the ads, but this stricture was circumvented by Borismasters when they started gaining ads in 2014.** *Matthew Wharmby*

case with a renewal date of 22 February 2014. For the moment, E 57 was treated to accident repairs at Hants & Dorset as Peckham's Es continued to proceed through.

In September Stockwell Es 62 and 63 were transferred to Bexleyheath for the 132 alongside ageing PVLs, and the following month Es 64-66 joined them. This month saw E 205 given additions to its side ad for the film *Turbo* by which extra graphics were applied around the wheelarches and over the staircase panel, and in November E 263 was given an all-over ad luring travellers to Mexico; it lasted two months. Seven Peckham Es were refurbished in October and four more by December.

It appeared that no further Enviro400s were on the menu for Go-Ahead London after the sheer glut of them in recent years, but the order placed for three for March

delivery was as different again from current specifications as could be imagined. Not only to 10.9m length but featuring, for the first time on a London-spec E40D, bonded glazing, Es 281-283 were intended for the Commercial Services department, which until now had always been composed of older buses coming out of stage service. This meant that the original red and grey-skirt livery would return, plus the white band Commercial Services had adopted. And that would be the end of the Enviro400 as we knew it, given the unveiling in May of the MMC version with substantial external differences.

With the completion of refurbishments to the Peckham batch of Es, the ENs based at Northumberland Park for the 231 began to stage through Hants & Dorset in February 2014, necessitating loans of WVLs to free them up. The lone E 276 was sighted once each on the 20 and 257, away from its normal work. While hybrids had become a fixture in London with the help of large wads of grant money, the methods by which braking energy would be stored were beginning to move away from heavy and just as polluting banks of batteries to a flywheel-based system. WVL 243 at Camberwell had already been fitted with a Williams Gyrodrive system and in February fellow Camberwell E 112 was so fitted for comparison.

E 265 gained all-over ad livery for *Rio 2* in March, this deal lasting two months. E 219 reverted to red (ex-Lycamobile) in June and E 268 gained a scheme for iBus, which was more like a partial ad in that the emphasis was towards the back, which was 'hollowed out' to reveal clockwork workings (now that would be emission-free!). And finally, to bring its vehicles into line with the contract term, the 486's Es started undergoing refurbishment in the summer, E 39 going first and five more done by September.

Carnival augmentation 36X this year was operated, as in 2013, by New Cross with Es and EHs.

Below: **Probably the last Enviro400s of London General or Central in the familiar form before the new MMC design are the three long-wheelbase examples taken in 2014 by the Commercial Services Department. On 13 April 2014 E 282 (YX14 RTZ) has taken itself to Brooklands.**
Matthew Wharmby

During 2014 the 453 was selected for conversion to Borismaster (LT) operation, and when this occurred in November the Mandela Way Es were progressively displaced to Camberwell where they replaced the WVL 212-273 batch of Volvo B7TLs from the 68 and 468; those Volvos that did not top up existing allocations group-wide made a new venture at Metrobus on the 161, where they saw off ageing Scanias. The last E at Mandela Way was E 175, which operated on the 1 on 23 December. In December E 246 lost its Rimmel ad.

2015 opened with overcrowding problems arising to London Bridge station, and as part of alleviation exercises, three local routes

Above: **The much-truncated but still important 68 received a new face towards the end of 2014, as Es displaced its WVLs after eight years. Formerly belonging to Mandela Way but displaced from there to Camberwell by a Borismaster is E 189 (SN61 BJJ), crossing Waterloo Bridge on 3 December 2014.**
Matthew Wharmby

Right: **Since its win by London Central the X68 has been resolutely WVL-operated, using vehicles from the main batch for the 68 and 468, but once the Volvos started to leave Camberwell, existing Enviro400s stepped up. At Waterloo on 3 December 2014 is E 103 (LX09 EZZ) from the 345's batch.**
Matthew Wharmby

Left: **All of Camberwell's double-deck routes now see Es from the 453's former batch; here at Clapham Junction on 18 January 2015 is E 185 (SN61 BHY) on the perennially busy inner-city route 345.**
Matthew Wharmby

Left: **The 185 is probably better known for the troubles it suffered in recent years when its operator London Easylink collapsed and a myriad of companies had to sweep in on an emergency basis with all sorts of buses. After that, East Thames Buses settled down with the contract, following which this company was sold by TfL to Go-Ahead. In due course the 185 was reallocated to Camberwell and its ex-London Easylink and East Thames Buses VPs replaced with WVLs leaving the 11. However, now that the 453's original Es have taken over from WVLs on the 68 and 468, appearances on the 185 are possible, like that of E 195 (SN61 BJY) at Catford on 17 February 2015.**
Matthew Wharmby

Left: **The 45 alone was not designated for new buses, the stock that replaced its AVLs comprising refurbished PVLs made spare from the loss of the 35 and 40 to Travel London in 2009. Still, 61-reg Es now turn out when convenient, exemplified at Brixton on 12 April by E 168 (SN61 BGX).**
Matthew Wharmby

were handed augmentations. One was the 21, on which Commercial Services E 281 was one of many buses to make an appearance.

Hybrid technology was by this time progressing from the battery concept to a new development involving flywheels, and to this end EN 13 was sent to GKN in Telford for fitment thus; it was replaced at Northumberland Park by E 94, transferred up from New Cross.

Pepsi undertook a big push in 2015, their Pepsi Max drink appearing on London Central Es 35 and 214 in February. At the same time, TfL was trumpeting its own ecological achievements with a scheme called Green Bus, built around a foliage motif and applied in this case to EH 17.

On 4 April London General took the 432 from Arriva London South; Stockwell WVLs were joined in the PM peak by a single Camberwell E cross-worked from the 468.

A new E allocation started at Silvertown (SI) on 20 May when Docklands Buses prepared for the takeover of the 135 (from the 23rd) with Es moved out of New Cross following their displacement from the 436 by WHVs ejected from the 12 by Borismasters. Although the 135 was intended

for new EHVs, most of its drivers would be TUPEd from Arriva and thus were used to Enviro400s. They also appeared on the D7 and 673. Once the 135's new EHVs had arrived and had bedded themselves in, the stopgap Es were moved out; first they were put into action on the Wimbledon tennis services between 29 June and 12 July, plus the Hampton Court Flower Show service, but their subsequent deployment proved a surprise when on 10 July an E was sighted on the 127 out of Metrobus's Croydon depot. This route was earmarked for new buses as it

was, but WVLs had been the last type moved to cement Metrobus's gradual folding into London General's identity within Go-Ahead.

Not only did the 127 take Es (and permit swift appearances on the 119 and 293), but Orpington collected five Es to spread around the 126, 161, 246, 320, 353, 654 and R9; the balance from the E 208-223 batch topped up Peckham and Stockwell (one each), Camberwell (two) and Bexleyheath (three).

In May E 214 resumed red livery, and in June EH 17 exchanged its Green Bus advert for a Sony PS4 one.

Above: **Bexleyheath's E fleet grew in the autumn of 2015 when the 88's original batch of Es transferred in following the replacement of that route's subequent EHs by Borismasters. Seen at Eltham on 18 October is E 129 (SN60 BZA).** *Matthew Wharmby*

London's latest Borismaster conversion was the 88, slotted in somewhat unexpectedly, and from 22 August the new LTs into Stockwell began displacing the route's EHs to the 87, for which they had been intended in the first place, and in turn sending the garage's complement of 60-reg Es to Bexleyheath to replace Go-Ahead's last Euro 2-engined buses, the refurbished PVLs that had been sharing the 132 with the previous intake of ex-Stockwell Es. EH appearances on the 19 began from shortly after this point.

During the summer the first five EHs underwent refurbishment, losing their green leaves in the process. E 35 lost its Pepsi Max ad at the same time (July). Repaints to Bexleyheath's original contingent of Es progressed during August.

During the Tube strike day of 9 July, Blue Triangle despatched two of their Enviro400s to help out in town; EN 25 on the 11 and EN 26 on the 14.

Since the delivery of E 283 a lull had affected the Enviro400 within Go-Ahead

Right: **Stockwell's 13-reg EHs officially moved from the 88 to the 87 once Borismasters arrived for the former, but were apt to wander to the 337 as well, as evinced by EH 28 (YX13 BJY) heading back to the garage from Clapham Junction on 12 November 2015.** *Matthew Wharmby*

Above: **The 87 is not by any means the powerhouse that its predecessor, the 77A, once was, and tends to operate the leavings of Stockwell's fleet. However, once Borismasters had taken over the 88 in the autumn of 2015, the 87 received its rightful complement of hybrids. EH 38 (YX13 BJY) draws up to Westminster station on 10 October.** *Matthew Wharmby*

Left: **Faithful to the 337 from their delivery, the small batch of 11-reg Es was progressively broken up in 2014 and 2015; in December Es 156 and 157 were sent to Sutton for a PVR boost in accordance with its retained contract. On 7 December E 157 (SN11 BUJ) sets off from Kingston. Upon the arrival of WHVs at Sutton in January 2016, both buses returned to Stockwell.** *Matthew Wharmby*

following the company's receipt of Volvo B5LHs and Borismasters, but in October, to furnish the winning back of the 35 and 40 from Abellio from April 2016, 22 more EHs were ordered. This time they would be to the MMC style, and would be joining the company's first MCV-bodied vehicles in the form of MHV-class Volvo B5LHs.

Two ad changes were manifest during October 2015; E 262 to a scheme for online food delivery service Hungry House (carried until January) and EH 17 from PS4 to red.

In November Es 282 and 283 with the Commercial Services fleet were reallocated from Sutton to Metrobus's Croydon. EH 15 was given a Green Bus ad in the same month.

During the autumn and into what passed for winter this year, Es began to turn out in sizeable numbers on the 12, while New Cross's Es wandered with regularity from the 36 to the 21.

The company's Es are to shuffle considerably during 2016, the first ones to move being the 68's when they were displaced by Borismasters starting on 6 February. Four 61-reg Es immediately left for

Above: **The elegant original livery of Go-Ahead's Es shows no signs of disappearing any time soon, though all of its original carriers at Bexleyheath have now been repainted and inroads are being made into those now at Merton. Next in line age-wise are the 09-reg Es new to Stockwell for the 345 but subsequently moved with the route to Camberwell, where they remain. This Waterloo shot of E 117 (LX09 FBJ) on 11 February 2016 comes five days after the conversion of the 68 route to Borismaster had commenced, but it was to be the 61-reg Es selected to leave Camberwell for pastures new.** *Matthew Wharmby*

Left: **Merton's runout is so large and diverse that more or less anything can appear on the 44, 77 and 270; here at Tooting on 23 February 2016 is E 86 (LX57 CKV), new to Stockwell for the 24.** *Matthew Wharmby*

Above: **Temporary route 541,
which had become rather
more permanent a fixture in
recent months due to ongoing
Crossrail work in its catchment
area, was reactivated again
on 15 February 2016 and this
time was the province of Es
released from Camberwell by
the conversion of the 68 to
Borismaster. On 18 February
at Canning Town E 175
(SN61 BHF) is on attachment
to Docklands Buses' Silvertown
garage, but is making do with
a windscreen slipboard in lieu
of blinds.** *Matthew Wharmby*

Belvedere, there to be prepared for transfer to Metrobus Croydon to see off that company's last 03-reg Scanias in the 400s block, alongside an incongruous allocation of ex-Bexleyheath PVLs that thus gave Croydon a sixth type allocated! Four more passed to Silvertown to serve as the temporary 541's allocation upon its reactivation from 15-19 February.

The big surprise was the transfer of ENs 25-27 to Bexleyheath to complete the Enviro400 complement on the 132 after its balance of

Euro 3 PVLs finally suffered expiry of the grace period allotted them since the start of 3016.

Although exact dispositions are not yet finalised at the time this book went to press, allocations will be needed variously at Silvertown, which will be taking the 147 from from Stagecoach on 7 May) and at Merton (route 57 to come from London United on 2 July). At least some should be coming from the 345 when it's lost to Abellio on 30 April).

Registrations

E 1-15	SN06 BNA/B/D-F/J-L/O/U/V/X-Z
E 16-39	LX06 EZL-P/R-T, EYY/Z, EZA-H, ECT/V, FKL-O
E 40-56	LX56 ETD-F/J-L/O/R/T-V/Y/Z, EUA-D
E 57-61	LX07 BYH/C/D/F/G
E 62-93	LX57 CHV/Y/Z, CJE/F/J/O/U/V/Y/Z, CKA/C-G/J-N-P/U/V/Y, CLF/J/N/O/V/Y
E 94-99	LX08 EBP/U/V/Z, ECA
E 100-128	LX09 EZU-W/Z, FAF/J/M/O/U, FBA-G/J/K/N/O/U/V/X/Y, FCA/C-E
E 129-150	SN60 BZA-H/J-M/O/P/R-Y
E 151-162	SN11 BTZ, BUA/E/F/H/J/O/P/U/V/W
E 163-204	SN61 BGF/K/O/U/V/X-Z, BHA/D, BGE, BHE/F/J-L/O/P/U-Z, BJE/F/JK/O/U/V/X-Z, BKA/D-G/J-L
E 205-228	SN61 DCV/X-Z, DDA/E/F/J-L/O/U/V/X-Z, DEU, DFA/C-G/J
E 229-245	YX61 DSV/O/V/Y/Z, DTF/K/N, DPF/K/N/O/U/V/Y/Z
E 246-260	YX12 FPA/C-G/J-L/N-P/T-V
E 261-275	SN62 DDE/O/X, DFL/X, DGF/U, DHA/X/Z, DJO, DKJ, DLY/Z, DMV
E 276-280	SN13 CJE/F/J/O/U
E 281-283	YX14 RTV/Z, RUA
EH 1-5	LX58 DDJ/K-O
EH 6-20	SN61 BLJ/K/V, DAA/O/U, DBO/V/X-Z, DCE/O/U
EH 21-38	YX13 BJE/F/J/K/O/U/V/Y/Z, BKA/D-G/J-L/N

Date:	Deliveries:	Licensed for service:
04.06	E 1, 4, 6-12	
05.06	E 2, 3, 5, 13-22, 27-30	E 1-15 (**SW**)
06.06	E 23-26, 31-36	E 16-36 (**PM**)
07.06	E 37-39	E 37 (**PM**), E 38, 39 (**SW**)
01.07	E 40-45	
02.07	E 46-56	E 40-56 (**BX**)
03.07	E 57	E 57 (**SW**)
06.07	E 58-61	E 58-61 (**A**)
10.07	E 62-93	
11.07		E 62-78, 82-93 (**SW**)
12.07		E 79-81 (**SW**)
04.08	E 94-99	E 94-99 (**NX**)
12.08	EH 1	
01.09	EH 2-5	EH 1-5 (**SW**)
06.09	E 100-119	E 100-108, 110-115 (**SW**)
07.09	E 120-128	E 116-124 (**SW**)
08.09		E 125-128 (**SW**)
10.10	E 129-137	E 129-137 (**SW**)
12.10	E 138-148	E 138-141 (**AL**)
01.11	E 149, 150	
02.11		E 142-150 (**AL**)
05.11	E 151-162	E 151-162 (**SW**)
08.11	E 163-174	E 163-166, 168-173 (**MW**)
09.11	E 175-190	E 167, 174-187 (**MW**)
10.11	E 191-208, EH 6-13	E 188-201 (**MW**), E 202-207 (**BX**), E 208 (**NX**), EH 6-11 (**NX**)
11.11	E 209-228, EH 14-20	E 209-228 (**NX**), EH 12-20 (**NX**)
01.12	E 229-245	E 229-245 (**BX**)
06.12	E 246-260	
08.12		E 246-260 (**BX**)
01.13	E 261-275	E 261-275 (**NX**)
05.13	E 276-280, EH 21-37	E 276 (**NP**), E 277-280 (**AL**), EH 21-37 (**SW**)
06.13	EH 38	EH 38 (**SW**)
03.14	E 281-283	E 281 (**NX**), E 282, 283 (**A**)

Acquired

31.03.12	EN 1-24 from First London
22.06.13	EN 25-27 from First London

Abellio London

9401-9558, 2401-2533

By the time Travel London was awarded the contract for new route 452 in the middle of 2006, with a December start date, this company was in its second incarnation, having grown to its extent by purchasing the operations of both Limebourne and Connex Bus. Therefore it was in a healthier position to grow than Connex, which had underbid on its contracts and struggled.

The 452 was conceived in order to take on the passengers that TfL perceived would be deterred from coming into central London by the western extension of the Congestion Charge. Following the 52 from Kensal Rise south as far as Knightsbridge station, it then turned off to follow the 137, terminating at Wandsworth Road station and thus circumnavigating the western edge of the zone.

The 452 was to have a PVR of 20, with reductions to the 52 and 137, but in order to include some buses for a top-up to the 3, Travel London placed an order in late June for 27 Alexander Dennis Enviro400s.

Upon the takeover of Tellings-Golden Miller, Travel London renumbered its combined fleet into a common series with

Below: **Seen at Ladbroke Grove on 3 March 2007 is Battersea's ED 11 (LJ56 VTN) when brand new. Shortly afterwards, it would assume the fleetnumber 9411.** *Matthew Wharmby*

traditional class codes, and that chosen for the Enviro400s was ED. The 452, however, was intended to commence on 2 December 2006, some time before the new buses were due, and indeed made its bow with existing Tridents of TA class, based out of Battersea (QB) garage.

The first examples were delivered on 9 January and ten were in stock by the end of the month. Their service debut came on Monday 22 January when ED 1 performed as QB233 and ED 4 QB237. On the 15th and 16th ED 3 was lent to Quality Line (Epsom Buses) for route trials along routes 406 and 418 in advance of that company's delivery of ten of their own Enviro400s.

The extra EDs in the order had their role switched as deliveries progressed; they would now be added to the 344, displacing five of its Vs (long-wheelbase Volvo B7TLs) to the 3 instead. All 27 were in service by the end of March, just about in time for the Western Extension of the Congestion Charge to be put into action on 19 February 2007. The last ten of them were delivered as 56-registrations gave way to 07-registrations from 1 March and received new plates accordingly.

The ED class codes were barely in place a month before another fleetwide renumbering exercise took place, this time with four-figure numeric identities to fit in with parent company Travel West Midlands. Accordingly, officially from 10 March EDs 1-27 became 9401-9427, leaving at least a bit of room before Volvo B7TLs (Vs) commenced at 9701.

ED 27 (to be 9427) was the last delivered and was a guest at this year's Cobham rally, held at Longcross. Though scheduled for the 452 and 344, EDs immediately began to wander, turning up on the 156 and 211. The new all-numeric fleetnumbers were applied by May.

That was it for the moment, the only excitement between the delivery of Travel London's first Enviro400s and the company's bid for the 35 and 40 being the appearance of two on the 188 (a Walworth route) on 23 February 2008, and one more on 27 March.

Below: **The rear aspect of the Travel London ED class of Enviro400 is shown by ED 9 (LJ56 VTL) a little further to the south of where the previous picture was taken on the same day.** *Matthew Wharmby*

Left: **Bravely trying to attract attention away from RMC 1469 and RLH 23 on 1 April 2007 at Longcross is ED 27 (LJ07 OPM), the last of the 452's batch and one of several to have to surrender their booked 56-registrations for new '07' marks.** *Matthew Wharmby*

In September 2008 Travel London was awarded the 35 (plus night route N35) and 40, and together with the renewed contract on the 156 was set to triple its Enviro400 fleet, ordering fifty-seven for spring 2009 delivery.

The new acquisitions would be split over the company's premises, the 40 operating out of Walworth and the 35 and 156 from what was shortly to be a vastly expanded Battersea.

9413 was the lone E400 to work alongside four 'TAs' and three loaned Metroline Tridents (DTs) on a service linking Canning Town with the ExCel on 10-13 November 2008. By the end of the year 'EDs' had racked up the 381, and iBus was fitted to all company vehicles by the first half of January 2009.

When the announcement was made that the 344 had been retained on tender, twenty more Enviro400s were added to the ongoing order, making a total of 77. The thirty-nine of these needed for the 35 and 40 started arriving in March 2009, but until the

assumption of the routes on 2 May they were stored at Beddington Cross and Fulwell. Nos 9428-9445 were allocated to Walworth for the 40 and 9446-9466 to Battersea for the 35, and Walworth's examples could immediately begin turning out on the 188. Unlike the first 27, this batch had a new interior decor with grey seat moquette.

On 21 May National Express sold Travel London and its Surrey offshoot Travel Surrey to NedRailways for £32m, with no plans as yet to change fleetnames (though that would prove to be exactly what happened!)

Contract renewal dates for two Travel London routes awaiting E400s were 22 August (route 344) and 12 September (route 156). The former's buses comprised nos 9467-9486 and the latter's 9487-9504, all to Euro 5 specification with ZF Ecolife six-speed gearboxes. In May the 414 was won from First London for a 21 November takeup and nineteen more Enviro400s ordered. In build from June onwards, the new buses were delivered between July and September but entered service slowly due to the need to fit iBus equipment to them, which had to come from the Tridents they replaced. 9504 didn't make it in time to retain its booked 09-plate (LJ09 OLV) and was re-registered LF59 XDZ, though it went around for about a week carrying the cancelled original mark! Two-thirds of the new buses were in place at Battersea by October and all were in service by the 28th of that month.

NedRailways now rebranded the operations Abellio London and Abellio Surrey, matching the name used by the German operations and meaning as much (or as little) in that language as it does in English. Formal unveiling of the new identity and its rather weedy accompanying fleetname was on 30 October, though Travel London fleetnames were progressively removed from the last few days of September onwards. The legal identities followed suit with effect from 1 June 2010.

The 414's batch was up next, and a change was evident here in that Edinburgh registrations were now specified, the manufacturers registering the vehicles themselves and gradually ensuring that

London marks would actually become extremely rare on the buses serving the capital. 9505-9523 were delivered in November and entered service on the 21st. With nearly a hundred Enviro400s now based, the fully revamped and purpose-built Battersea could put spares out where needed, and the C3 became the latest occasional user of the type, with corresponding visits by 'Vs' to E400-operated routes.

2010 proved quiet after a busy 2009, and indeed two of Abellio's routes were retained on tender in the form of the 188 and 343 with their existing Volvo B7TLs; one fresh acquisition was the 172, but this was to be set going with acquired second-hand Tridents displaced from Armchair and put through refurbishment. Naturally, E400s could be counted upon to turn out on the 172 and were soon doing so in some numbers.

In March 2011 an order was placed for thirteen Enviro400 hybrids, which would be allocated to the 188 alongside existing but refurbished Volvo B7TLs. This was part of the first allocation to London companies under the auspcies of the Government's Green Bus Fund. At the moment their fleetnumbers were pencilled in as 2001-2013. However, Abellio went on to place an additional order off its own bat, intending to restock the 3 with twenty-four of them from February 2012.

The all-over advert wrap came to Abellio for the first time in May 2011, Battersea's 9504 and 9523 taking on schemes advertising tourism to Malaysia; they lasted three months.

2012 was certainly set to be a banner year for Abellio London and for the Enviro400, because not only was the 211 retained with the promise of new diesel-engined examples but the C2 was won from Metroline for takeup on 28 April 2012; an order for 35 Enviro400s

and six hybrids was placed. With the coming of the European Community Whole Vehicle Type Approval regulations, emissions alterations were made to various chassis in order to meet these new needs, and the Enviro400 type was redesignated E40D (for diesel) and E40H (for hybrid). The six of the latter were to form a partial allocation on the 211, a common strategy where there wasn't yet a viable difference between the price of a full set of hybrids if not subsidised wholly or partly by Government. Popular opinion was being steered towards reducing emissions in central London as a priority, leading to trunk routes there going over to hybrids first.

The 188's hybrids started delivery in December, numbered 2401 up for alleged common purpose with the 9401+ numbers of their diesel counterparts, and straight after them came the 3's contingent as 2012 got going. Seating 61 (H37/24D), they weighed 11,950kg unladen. One was seen on the 188 on 13 January but only six were in service by the end of the month, the rest having to wait till February. With the onset of the new contract on the 3 and its night counterpart N3 on 11 February, the routes were reallocated from Beddington Cross to Battersea and 2414-2437 entered service from there. Appearances on the 40, 156, 344 and C3 soon followed. They weighed 11915 kg, a little less than the first thirteen, but weight was becoming

a serious issue on modern buses as a whole, as legislation compelled them to take on item after item, all of which added weight at the expense of fuel capacity and thus the ability to license an optimum number of passengers; official standing capacity was what ended up being pruned.

On 12 March the C2's batch of E40Ds began delivery and were stored at Battersea, some entering service on other routes from the garage from the 10th until the C2 was assumed on the 28th. It took only two days before a hybrid visited the C2, and in general they could be seen on anything at any time; any bus rather than no bus! Half the 211's E40Ds arrived and were licensed in June, followed over the rest of the month by the balance, plus the accompanying hybrids, and on 28 June came 9544, the Euro 6 prototype which due to its larger engine ended up being slightly longer and considerably heavier than its predecessors. Hybrid 2442 was fitted with Alexander Dennis's 'arrive and go' software update affecting the stop-start versus continuous running nature of the engine.

On 23 June the 35 and N35 were reallocated from Battersea to Walworth, taking with them 9446-9466.

Loosely related to the Olympics but designed to take sponsors' messages to as many possible customers as they could, four Enviros were given all-over ads in June; 9438 and 9444 for the Samsung Galaxy III and 9512 and 9513 for Vodafone. In July 9545 plus three Tridents were treated to a NedRail-related scheme for the Netherlands Olympic team, while 9412 became a Vodafone bus and 9507 and 9514 were set to tout Visa. 9434 was given a Vodafone ad in August.

Another lull ensued, only all-over ads breaking the quiet spell until more routes within range of Abellio's three garages came into the tendering arena. The Samsungs and Visas were restored to red by October, but a massive push by Apple of its latest iPod Touch iteration from November saw, amongst multiple other vehicles from numerous London companies, six Abellio Enviro400s treated; these were 9431, 9441, 9595, 9506, 9540 and 9543. The lowest two of these reverted to red within a month and the other four in January 2013.

Five years having passed since the company's first E400s had entered service on the 452, it was now time to refurbish that batch for their second term. 9420 was the pilot, coming back in April with Abellio's new red moquette fitted and yellow handrails, while the two-piece side blind was rationalised to a single aperture to accompany power blind fitment throughout. Inside, the handrail was removed from the wheelchair bay and lower saloon downseated from H41/26D to H41/24D. White-on-black blinds to the new TfL standard unveiled with the Borismaster reached Abellio during the year.

In June 2013 9519 received an all-over ad for Lycamobile; after a full year pushing Vodafone, 9512 and 9513 were restored to red that month. 9434 lost its Vodafone ad in July but 9477 gained one advertising McCain's oven chips, and in September 9516 was treated to a scheme warning against diabetes. October saw 9477 returned to red but 9406 and 9545 given another scheme for Malaysia, this time centred around the monkeys to be seen there and lasting for two months, while 9548 received this year's version of Poppy Day livery, enduring only for the duration of Remembrance Sunday. During November 9538 took an ad for the Taiwanese-made Asus T-100 notebook computer and 9554 one on behalf of Mexico City.

9401 suffered minor rear damage when part of the 22 September collision that wrecked LT 62 and damaged WHY 4, and

was not returned to service until the end of the year when it underwent refurbishment. 9510 was damaged by scaffolding falling on its roof but was repaired by 23 December.

Abellio's double-deck fortunes would stir in the year 2014, the company's first coup being something a long way out of what had become their geographic heartland but capable of being worked by the Hayes base inherited from Wing's Buses. This was the E1, the short and positively no-frills direct link from Ealing to Greenford. The second was much more significant; while substantially reduced from the extent of its heyday, the 49 was still a major route in west-central London and was within easy reach of two of its three main garages. To furnish them, plus the C3 retained on tender at the same time, an order was placed in December 2013 for 43 E40Hs, which would be delivered in three batches, one for each route (eight for the E1, 13 for the C3 and 22 for the 49).

January 2014 saw 9554 lose its Mexico City ad and 9538 give up its Asus ad. In February 9516 reverted to red but 9524 was given a scheme for Schuh schoes. Repaints

Above: **The 49 has bounced between several south London garages in its history, and Battersea (QB) could be said to be the spiritual heir of Hester Road. On 7 September 2014, the day after the takeover of the 49 by Abellio, we see 2472 (SN64 OEW) crossing Clapham Junction.** *Matthew Wharmby*

Right: **The way of the future, for Abellio and London's other Enviro400 operators, is the MMC (Major Model Change), with a radically redesigned front and an ethos that claims to be 'by the industry, for the industry'. Seen centre stage in Walworth garage's open day on 19 July 2014, the MMC prototype would eventually be registered YY64 GXG and go on the road.** *Matthew Wharmby*

started reaching the 09-registered batch this year, now that their 35 and 40 routes had been extended for two more years. 9510 was treated to an ad for *Spiderman 2* in April. This and 9524 reverted to red in May.

The E1 was slated to pass to Abellio on 31 May, but its new buses, 2444-2451, were run in on the 350 out of Hayes first. The allocation for the C3 followed straight after, comprising 2452-2464. However, much as with the award of London General's 87, the obsession with air quality in central London superseded the orderly deployment of hybrids to their intended route and this batch was spread over Battersea's existing routes operating closer to town instead, with the intent that they would be used predominantly on the 211. They entered service between 13-25 June.

There was a little breathing room until the 49 needed to start on 6 September, but the first two of its own batch were delivered on 27 June. As the rest arrived over July and August, the first two were licensed with 14-registrations and put into service early over a spread of Battersea-operated services. The batch constituted 2465-2486, and once registered from 1 September with 64-marks, were deployed in advance of the 49's takeover on the 6th; they were soon to be seen on any or all of Battersea's routes, with earlier hybrids and diesels returning the favour. The 414's batch of diesels, meanwhile, continued as their route was renewed for another five years from 22 November. Examples from the low 9500s range of stock numbers accordingly started going through refurbishment towards year's end.

One of the company's most important tendering victories was announced in May, that of the win of the 109 and 415 from Arriva London South for 2015 takeup. The 109, like the 49 a faded remnant of its former glory, was still a force to be reckoned with in south London, and with the strikingly pointless 415 as a makeweight would more than ensure the company's immediate future. It would also herald the first volume order by a London company for Alexander Dennis's E40D MMC, for Major Model Change. An early example of this top-to-toe redesign was taken by Abellio and displayed in red livery at its Walworth garage open day on 19 July 2014. For the 109 and 415, plus the one double-deck working on the 407 and finally the 350's retention announced in the summer, forty-five new E40H MMCs were ordered.

9519 lost its Lycamobile ad in July but was not red for long, receiving a Nokia Lumia 930 advert in August. No Abellio hybrids

Above: **Big changes are coming to the Elephant & Castle, transforming this dreary and dangerous inner-city arena to something the developers hope will be rather more upmarket. To that end the southern roundabout is now a more normal crossing, being negotiated on 12 April 2015 by Walworth's 9460 (LJ09 CDZ), and during that month major revamping of the northern roundabout commenced.**
Matthew Wharmby

Left: **A fair bit of mixing is inevitable now that Abellio can field over two hundred Enviro400s or Enviro400Hs; at Notting Hill Gate on 4 May 2015 we see 9547 (SN12 AOU), nominally purchased for the C2 but perfectly adequate on the 452 while that route's own 56-reg examples go through refurbishment.**
Matthew Wharmby

had yet been given all-over ads, so 2422 was the first when in October it gained a vinyl for the London Health Commission. Brand new 2460 followed it with this year's sparser Poppy Appeal livery, and in the same month 9545 was given a Mexico City scheme. 9406, after touting the Red Bull Culture Clash, was switched to advertising Malaysia. In December 9527, 9529 and 9530 gained ads for Candy Crush Saga, the addictive game.

The first orders for the MMC (Major Model Change) development of the Enviro400 in London were placed by Metroline to furnish the 332's contract, but they were beset by delivery delays and Abellio's order beat them into service. This top-to-toe redesign of the Enviro400 after nine years cost £7.5m and features a series of improvements both for the passenger, driver and engineer. As well as a staircase reduced in length by adding a square corner at the bottom, the MMC introduces quick-release gasket window pans, LED lighting and future adaptability to flywheel and electric propulsion. Overall there are weight savings and a resultant increase in fuel economy. All are to H41/25D capacity.

Abellio did very well for itself in 2014, winning the 109 and 415 for takeup early in 2015, and ordered 45 new MMC E40Hs.

Left: **Generally attractive-looking if a bit on the fussy side with its cut-out motifs and wide pillars obscuring the view out from the upper deck, the MMC entered service with Abellio London on 27 January 2015, the first examples being tried out on the 157 in advance of the 109's takeup on the 31st. On 1 February Beddington Cross's 2495 (YY64 TYT) is seen at West Croydon station on its way north.** Matthew Wharmby

Numbered 2487-2531, they were also for an upgrade and permanent double-deck conversion of the 350. They were the first MMCs to enter service, some being tried out on the 157 from 26 January 2015 before squadron entry on the 109 on the 31st, allocated to Beddington Cross. Nos 2487-2513 formed this route's allocation, and at night they worked the N109, similarly won from Arriva London South.

Next came the 415, taken over from Arriva London South's Norwood on 7 March and intended for 2515-2522 out of Walworth, but only two were available on the first day, so examples from the range 2401-2413 stood in, fitted in advance with blinds including the 415. To boost the allocation in any case, the demonstrator was taken on loan, now registered YY64 GXG and given the Abellio fleetnumber 2400, occupying the hybrids' series despite being a diesel E40D. This had begun work on the 381's peak-hour extras on 16 February, followed on the 21st by 2514, the first of the 415's MMCs on running-in.

Left: **The rear aspect of the MMC is demonstrated at West Croydon on 17 February 2015 by 2513 (YY64 TZN). The design is tidier than what its predecessor had evolved into, incorporating the myriad of exit grilles into a black theme which hopefully won't get gone over upon repaint. There is also a hint of 'hips' to the engine cowl, which is more daring an approach than Alexander Dennis tends towards.** Matthew Wharmby

Right: **Joining forces with the new MMC E40Hs on the 415 from 7 March was 2400 (YY64 GXG), the demonstration E40D already with an Abellio interior. It is seen at Brixton on 12 April 2015. At the northern end, the route was given a short extension from the Elephant & Castle to Old Kent Road Tesco.** *Matthew Wharmby*

Below: **Abellio's batch of MMC E40Hs were for three routes, and the third was the 350 linking Hayes & Harlington Station with Heathrow Terminal 5. Seen having set off from the former on 15 April 2015 is 2526 (YX15 OWU), with about the same number of passengers the route normally sees.** *Matthew Wharmby*

Not quite enough MMCs were available to man the 415 for its first week starting on 7 March, so E40Hs from the range 2401-2413 were fitted with blind sets including the route so as to be able to stand in.

Finally the 350 was added, its first examples seeing service from 21 March and comprising nos 2523-2531. These were based at Hayes, the former TGM depot.

On 17 January 2015 the 3 was temporarily

curtailed from the south to Regent Street, as part of a programme of short-term cutbacks to mitigate roadworks in connection with Crossrail construction.

In February 9419 was treated to an all-over ad for Pepsi Max, and during March 2460 (ex-Poppy Appeal) and 9524 and 9526 (ex-Candy Crush) reverted to red. On 16 March Battersea's 2429 incurred frontal damage after hitting a wall while on the 344; it was repaired and returned to service on 23 May.

April saw 9406, 9529, 9530 and 9545 resume all-red, but 9527 swapped its Candy Crush ad for a new one advertising Crocs footwear under the banner 'Find your fun'. 2422 returned to red in May.

During June 2516 and 2517 swapped identities due to a paperwork mixup with chassis and body numbers vis-a-vis the registrations booked for each. During that

month 9419 regained red livery (ex-Pepsi Max) and 9519 exchanged its Nokia Lumia ad for one for Sunglass Hut.

Two further E40H MMCs were 2532 and 2533 intended for the increased PVR on the 415 following its extension to Old Kent Road Tesco. 2533 was delivered on 8 July, 2532 on the 10th and they entered service soon after at Walworth, though 2400 didn't move on as was intended.

July saw 9525 and 9527 regain red livery (ex-Candy Crush and Crocs respectively). One of 2015's Poppy Appeal buses was 2460 between October and December, while 9519 resumed all-red in October.

2400's loan spell finally came to a close on 31 October, but it was quickly called back, this time out of Beddington Cross to cover for 2498, which on 10 November had suffered fire and smoke damage to its engine compartment while operating on the 109.

November's advert changes saw 9512 gain one for Hungry House and 9525 swap its Mexico scheme for one for clothing retailer Kit and Ace. This scheme made its way to 9550 in December.

Refurbishments to the 09-reg batch of Enviro400s began during December 2015.

Big things are due for Abellio's Enviro400 in 2016. Firstly, the 3 was converted to Borismaster starting on 9 February, freeing its hybrid E40Hs to take over the 381. The rest will go to the 344, where they will be joined in due course by twenty more E40H MMCs, and the existing E40Ds thus displaced from the 344 will head over to Hayes to take over the E9 on 28 May. That day will also see the 35 and 40 ceded to London Central in return for the 345, which will take their Enviro400s. By that time the intended conversion of the 211 to LT will have been completed in time to provide the buses needed. Eventually the great cascade of Enviro400s will see off all the company's remaining Tridents and no doubt begin making inroads into the Volvo B7TLs.

Registrations

ED 1-27	LJ56 VSZ, VTA/C-G/K-P/T-V, LJ07 OPE, LJ56 VTY, LJ07 OPF-H/K, LJ56 VUD, LJ07 OPL, LJ56 VUF, LJ07 OPE
9428-9466	LJ09 CAA/E/O/U/V/X, CBF/O/U/V/X/Y, CCA/D-F/K/N/O, CCU/X-Z, CDE/F/K/N/O/U/V/X-Z, CEA/F/K/N/O/U
9467-9503	LJ09 OJZ, OKA-H/K-P/R-W/X/Z, OLA-C/E/G/H/K/M-P/R/T/U
9504	LF59 XDZ
9505-9523	SN59 AVR/T-Z, AWA/C/F-J/M/O/P/R/U
9524-9543	SN12 AAV/X-Z, ABF/K/O/U/V/X/Z, ACF/J/O/U/V/X-Z, ADO
9544	SN12 AUO
9545-9558	SN12 AOS/T-Z, APF/K/O/U/V/X
2401-2413	SN61 DFL/O/P/U/V/X-Z, DGE/F/O/U/V
2414-2437	SN61 DGX-Z, CXX-Z, CYA/C/E-H/J-L/O/P/S-X
2438-2443	SN12 AUE/F/H/J-L
2444-2451	SK14 CTZ, CUA/C/G/H, SYY, SYZ, SZC
2452-2464	SL14 DDF/J/K/N/O/U/V/X/Y/Z, DEU, DFA, DFC
2465-2466	SL14 LOA, LOD
2467-2486	SN64 OER-Z, OFA-E/G/H/J-M
2487-2514	YY64 TYD/F-H/K/O/P/S-Z, TZA-H/J-O
2515-2533	YX15 OWD-H/J/K/M/O/P/R/U-W/Y/Z, OXA-C

Date:	Deliveries:	Licensed for service:
01.07	ED 1-10	ED 1, 2, 4-6 (**QB**)
02.07	ED 11, 17, 19, 24, 26	ED 3, 7-14, 16, 17, 26 (**QB**)
03.07	ED 18, 20-23, 25, 27	ED 15, 18-25, 27 (**QB**)
03.09	9428-9455	
04.09	9456-9466	
05.09		9428-9445 (**WL**), 9446-9466 (**QB**)
07.09	9467-9478	
08.09	9479-9493	9467-9470, 9472 (**QB**)
09.09	9494-9504	9471, 9473-9492, 9494 (**QB**)
10.09		9493, 9495-9504 (**QB**)
11.09	9505-9523	9505-9523 (**QB**)
12.11	2401-2409, 2411, 2412	
01.12	2410, 2413-2437	2402-2407 (**WL**)
02.12		2401, 2408-2412 (**WL**), 2414-2437 (**QB**)
03.12	9524-9543	
04.12		9524-9543 (**QB**)
05.12	9545-9553	
06.12	9544, 9554-9558, 2438-2443	9544-9558, 2438-2443 (**QB**)
05.14	2444-2451	2444-2451 (**WS**)
06.14	2452-2466	2452-2464 (**QB**)
07.14	2467-2472	
08.14	2473-2486	2465, 2466 (**QB**)
09.14		2467-2486 (**QB**)
12.14	2487-2498	
01.15	2499-2514	2487-2513 (**BC**), 2514 (**WL**)
02.15	2515-2519	
03.15	2520-2528	2515-2522 (**WL**), 2523-2528 (**WS**)
04.15	2529-2531	2529-2531 (**WS**)
07.15	2532, 2533	2532, 2533 (**WL**)

Loaned from Alexander Dennis Ltd, 12.14:
2400 (YY64 GXG), ADL E40D H41/25D

Arriva Kent Thameside

6458-6470, T 301-331

By 2011, route 160 was one of just two TfL double-deck routes operated by Arriva Kent Thameside despite a long history of running such services for London Buses and LRT since Kentish Bus days. The thirteen Y-registered 'DLAs' in residence were due for replacement in 2012 and towards the end of 2011 thirteen E40Ds were ordered, to be numbered 6458-6470.

They commenced delivery on 23 December with eight in stock by New Year's Eve, and even before the rest had arrived, the first two entered service on 3 January 2012. Curiously, the gap between deliveries meant that the remainder, which arrived over January, were registered with Northampton marks where 6458-6465 bore the Maidstone plates you would expect to see in this part of the world. They were to H41/24D capacity and weighed 11,655kg, and all were in service by 25 January.

The only variety possible with this one-route batch is visits to the 492, which are performed on a fairly regular basis.

After a very long impasse, things stirred again at this company during the autumn

of 2015 when the 229 was awarded from London Central. For this plus the retention of the 492 from 23 January 2016, 31 E40Ds were ordered. To the original style of body, these were allotted the numbers 6485-6515, but by the end of the year plans had changed to reflect the increasing assimilation of the outer London operations into the main Arriva London network. On the one hand, this thankfully brought back class codes in the traditional London manner, but on the other hand, the lazy practice of number skipping was repeated with numbers to resume from T 301 rather than the more logical and sensible T 285. Still, there is logic in the leaving of a gap, because with the plan, 6458-6470 are to become Ts 288-300. The transfer will formally take effect later in 2016.

Above: **Dartford's 6470 (KX61 LDV) sets off from Bluewater during the late afternoon of 8 September 2012; the 492 was normally Wright-bodied DAF (or VDL) DB250RS(LF)s identical to the DW class at Arriva London South.** *Matthew Wharmby*

Left: **To all intents and purposes, the E40Ds new in January 2016 were traditional London buses, with their T class codes. Dartford's T 301 (LK65 ENN) and partners took over the 229 from London Central on 23 January, and is seen on the 25th at Sidcup Station.** *Matthew Wharmby*

Right: **On 18 February 2016 T 318 (LK65 ENJ) approaches Bexleyheath.** *Matthew Wharmby*

Right: **It took a little longer for the 492 to get all its E40Ds, but they were all in place by mid-February; here on the eastern edge of Bexleyheath on 18 February is T 315 (LK65 ENE).** *Matthew Wharmby*

Registrations

6458-6465	GN61 JPY, JSV, JRV, JRX, JRO, JRZ, JSU, JRU
6466-6470	KX61 LDL/N/O/U/V
T 301-331	LK65 ENN-P/R/T-Y, EMJ/V/X, ENC/E/F/H/J/L/M, EKZ, ELC/H/J/O/U-X, EMF, EKN

Date	Deliveries	Licensed for Service
12.11	6458-6465	
01.12	6466-6470	6458-6470 (**DT**)
12.15	T 301-308	
01.16	T 309-319, 321-325, 327-331	T 301-319, 321-325, 327-331 (**DT**)
02.16	T 320, 326	T 320, 326 (**DT**)

6458-6470 to be renumbered T 288-300 upon their company's transfer to Arriva London North, 2016

Arriva the Shires

5448

Always on the fringes of red bus operation but never quite a part of it, Arriva the Shires was taking the same kinds of vehicles as its London cousins though numbering them in its own numeric series, thus employing 'DLAs' on the 142 and 340 and 'DWs' on the 258. When Arriva London North finally tried out the Enviro400 and classified them T, Arriva the Shires took one too, the one-off 5448. It entered service on 3 March 2012 out of Garston, and there it remains, helping out on the 142, 340 and 642.

The transfer of Arriva the Shires' London operations to Arriva London North portends a renumbering for Garston's only Enviro400, which will rechristen 5448 to T 199.

Registration
5448   SN08 AAE

Date	Delivery	Licensed for Service
02.08	5448	
03.08		5448 (**GR**)

To be renumbered T 199 upon its company's transfer to Arriva London North, 2016

Below: **Combining blacked-out window surrounds with the obsolete and disappearing yellow relief stripe of Arriva London is 5448 (SN08 AAE), setting off from Brent Cross on 28 July 2012.** *Matthew Wharmby*

London United

ADH 1-51, ADE 1-73

Under the stewardship of French-owned Transdev, London United had developed a distinct preference for the all-Polish Scania N230UD as its main double-decker, but when hybrids began to muscle onto the scene, investigated the Alexander Dennis Enviro400H cautiously when two from the preliminary order were allocated to join the existing SPs on the 482, a new route introduced on 22 March 2008 to replace the 435.

Coded ADH and seating 63 (H37/26D), the duo arrived in the first week of January 2009 and went into service on the 22nd of that month. They bore the cheerful plethora of green leaves over their basic red, which added colour and suitably touted their green credentials. Operation proved stable enough to risk transferring out two SPs in July.

London United kept hold of the 94 on tender, having operated it with TLA-class Tridents since its OPO conversion, and a punt was taken on upgrading as much of the route as possible to hybrid operation by allocating it twenty of the next order for Enviro400Hs from shortly after the contract renewal date of 16 October 2010. ADHs 3-22 were delivered during October and after

Below: **Looking smart in the early leafy version of hybrid livery, Hounslow Heath's ADH 2 (SN58 EOS), at Hatton Cross on 21 March 2010, is somewhat marred by the huge Transdev logo plastered over the front.**
Matthew Wharmby

preparation at Hounslow Heath (and the display of ADE 9 at the LT Museum's Acton Open Day and of ADE 10 at Euro Bus Expo) entered service from 4 November, displacing about two-thirds of the TLAs. This time the branding was more subdued, only a stylised 'hybrid' wording incorporating a sprouting leaf being used, and logos didn't appear until February 2011. Two seats had been deleted from the specification this time, affording a H37/24D capacity.

On 3 March London United was taken over by RATP and new logos began to make their appearance. The only wandering of this class so far was of Shepherd's Bush's batch to the H91 while that route was based there, but a little later examples tried out the 220 as well.

Three of London United's most important local services were up for tender during 2011, and in September it was announced that the company had retained the 120, to be followed in October by the retention of the 81 and 222. All required new vehicles for summer 2012 introduction, the 222 additionally gaining an upgrade to full double-deck operation. However, the supply of Polish Scanias had run dry following last orders for the type going to First for the 207, and for these routes a total of 45 Enviro400s was ordered, or more specifically the newly E40D-badged diesel variant. These would introduce the ADE class, and when the 220 was announced in December as staying with London United, 28 more were added in March. On 17 March 2012 the night service on that route was formally converted from TLA to ADH operation, using vehicles from the 94's daytime allocation.

Another round of Green Fund munificence was announced during 2012, and this time the beneficiary was to be the 27, operated since being taken back from First by Stamford Brook with SLEs and retained on tender from February 2012 with a 10 November start. In July an order was placed for twenty-nine further ADHs, and to standardise operations, ADHs 1 and 2 were expected to transfer to join their new counterparts.

The ADEs for the Hounslow-area routes commenced delivery on 12 June, in time for the 120's contract renewal date on the 23rd. ADEs 1-10 formed the partial upgrade for this route alongside existing SPs and entered service from Hounslow from the 21st. ADEs 11-25, the batch designated for the 81 (whose contract commenced on 28 July) were diverted to help out during the Olympics, providing extras on the 148 out of Shepherd's Bush so that its existing SPs could reinforce the 10. Almost at once a new ADE was given an all-over ad, this being ADE 12 promoting tourism to Brazil.

The 81's ADE allocation returned from their Olympic assistance from about 15 August and took up duty at Hounslow, though the balance, once they had all arrived by 8 September, were stored at Hounslow Heath until the 222's start date on the 15th, and all were in service by that day. Five of them had to be re-registered with 62-plates, having gone past 1 September. Appearances soon ensued on the 111, H32 and H98, in Hounslow's time-honoured fashion!

Right: **Best remembered as the first route to go over to the private sector with second-hand DMSs, the 81 eventually returned to what became London United and has resumed full-time double-deck operation as the only carrier out of the western London borders past Heathrow and on to Slough. New ADEs formed the route's latest contract with London United, and on 12 May 2013 ADE 5 (YX12 FNL) circumnavigates the new and rather more attractive Slough bus station.**
Matthew Wharmby

Operating as they did through Oxford Street, the 94's ADHs soon became magnets for all-over ads; while ADE 12 was restored to red in August, ADH 5 and 6 gained schemes for Vodafone. ADE 2 also received this ad, while ADH 21 was given an ad for china manufacturers Royal Albert, which lasted till November. A crash in Regent Street on 14 September did not deter ADH 5. The type was taken further afield in June when ADH 13 made a trip to Paris to be displayed at the Transports Publics roadshow.

The 220's new five-year term commenced on 20 October, and from the end of September its new ADEs started piling up at Hounslow Heath. However, a late change reallocated the route from its historic Shepherd's Bush base to the former NCP Challenger garage at Park Royal, though when ADEs started entering service on 5 October it was from Shepherd's Bush, which was used to the class after its forays to the 148 during the Olympics. While at Shepherd's Bush, one ADE crept out on the 94. The 49 added itself to the possibilities for Shepherd's Bush ADH wanderings, meanwhile.

A big push by Apple saw multiple buses liveried for its iPod; November saw ADE 12 and ADHs 4, 7 and 8 treated. ADE 12's scheme lasted only a month and the iPod campaign was concluded by mid-January.

The final development so far concerning London United's ADH and ADE classes came on 10 November with the renewal of the 27's contract, adding an extension on this date from Turnham Green to Chiswick Business Park, site of the much-missed London Transport Chiswick Works. In advance of conversion of the route to hybrids, ADHs 1 and 2 left Hounslow Heath on 9 November,

Middle and right: **Two of the 45-strong ADE complement added to Hounslow in 2013 for routes 81, 120 and 222; ADE 4 (YX12 FNK) on 6 May 2013 and ADE 32 (YX12 GHU) on 10 June 2014, photographed at either end of Hounslow town centre.** *Matthew Wharmby*

but until the rest arrived were allocated from 5 December to Shepherd's Bush to support the 94's existing complement. On 14 January 2013 they were transferred to Stamford Brook and commenced from there the following day, by which time the 27's intended ADHs were in course of delivery. Service debut was on 25 January and all were in place by the beginning of March. They were fitted with the new 'Arrive and Go' system which cuts the engine below 4 mph and restarts it again at 7 mph, purporting to increase fuel savings by a further 6% beyond the 30-35% already enjoyed by hybrids. On 22 March the night service on the 10 was converted from SP to ADH operation using the 27's daytime buses, and strange workings now encompassed the 391, plus the 9 before its conversion later in the year to Borismaster (LT) operation, while Shepherd's Bush ADHs were apt to visit the 148. ADE 56 was deroofed under Old Oak Common railway bridge on 22 May, necessitating the loan of ADE 32 from Hounslow to Park Royal. ADH 10, meanwhile, hit the wall at Hammersmith bus station on 10 July.

Most developments up to publication date have comprised livery changes; ADH 14 was wrapped for Converse between March and June, when it received an ad for *Despicable Me 2*; ADH 12 was done in the same month for Lycamobile and lasted until August, by which time ADHs 5 and 6 were red again.

On 30 August 2013 ADEs 1-3 were loaned from Hounslow to Park Royal to bolster the 220 pending prolonged roadworks in Harlesden, which is a bottleneck as it is. When Borismasters onto the 9 started releasing vehicles in November, the resulting cascades saw three TAs added to Park Royal for this role.

In October ADH 14 was liveried for Malaysia's tourist drive and ADH 11 given a scheme for Fossil watches. ADH 15 also gained this scheme in November, which month also saw ADH 22 liveried to advertise Mexico tourism (till January) and seven route 94 ADHs (5, 6, 8, 19, 13, 16 and 19) wrapped in honour of the Asus T-100 laptop. These plus the Fossils were concluded by year's end, only for ADH 14 to take on yet another consecutive advert, this time for the Lord Mayor's Appeal. In March 2014 ADH 13 was liveried for Schuh shoes and ADH 16 for the movie *Rio 2*. Both lasted till May, when ADH

13 was given a scheme for McDonald's. In June ADH 12 was given a partial scheme for TfL's own iBus system. August saw ADH 10 wrapped for Rimmel (till December), ADH 13 exchanging its McDonald's ad for one for the Nokia Lumia 930 and ADH 15 taking a scheme for The Gap. In September ADH 12 traded its iBus piece for a Victoria's Secret wrap, and the following month ADHs 13 and 15 were rotated again, the former gaining this year's relatively lacklustre Poppy Appeal ad and the latter an ad exhorting Londoners to visit Puerto Vallarta in Mexico.

During June a temporary double-deck enhancement was applied to Hounslow's 203 during some roadworks, and ADEs participated. For the London Mela on 31 August Stamford Brook added four of its route 27 ADHs to the E3 for the day, normally the province of refurbished SPs since its acquisition from First.

The transfer of route 110 from Fulwell to Hounslow on 4 October 2014 brought the likelihood of ADE appearances, but the first one was not sighted until 18 December when ADE 44 did the honours. Sporadic visits followed into 2015.

Advert changes over the turn of 2014/15 restored Shepherd's Bush's ADH 10 to red in

Below: **In their short careers so far, the 94's ADHs have racked up seeming scores of all-over ads. Crossing Marble Arch on 11 October 2014 is Shepherd's Bush's ADH 13 (SN60 BYJ), advertising the Nokia Lumia 930 mobile phone.** *Matthew Wharmby*

Right: **The inconsistency and contradiction of the European Whole Vehicle Type specifications are remarkable. After generations of an offside emergency exit door, this is now unnecessary if vehicles are dual-doored, and so too has the opening rear upper-deck window become a fixed unit. Instead, hammers are carried for passengers to smash the windows if they need to get out, surely an irresponsible move in London where vandalism is an enjoyable and rarely punished pastime for many bus passengers. Here running short to Putney Bridge Station on 12 April is Park Royal-allocated ADE 68 (YX62 BPU).**
Matthew Wharmby

December (ex-Rimmel) and in January turned two of the Candy Crushes, ADHs 4 and 8, to ones for the Philippines. ADH 12 exchanged its Victoria's Secret ad for a Philippines one in the same month, and in March the other Candy Crush examples lost their ads, ADHs 5 and 13 resuming red livery and ADH 16 taking on a Peru advert intead. Routine repaints to ADHs were now on the cards, meanwhile, ADHs 1 and 15 going through the spray booth at Hants & Dorset during February, the latter (simultaneously losing its Mexico ad) receiving white fleetnumbers rather than the normal yellow.

Substitutions of Borismasters are rare, but now that their routes are predominantly OPO, not too many eyebrows are raised; accordingly ADH 42 turned out on the 9 on 5 February 2015.

Although Epsom Buses had been in the RATP group since purchase from the Richmond family in 2012, no moves had been made to federate its operations with London United, but on 31 March 2015 DD 15 was wrecked in a fatal accident on Penrhyn Road in Kingston and help was sought in the shape of ADE 45, loaned from Hounslow for use on the 406 and 418. It went home on 27 August.

Right: **The famous Chiswick Works, renowned for designing, building and overhauling so many London Transport buses, is no more, now just another anonymous business park, but since 31 May 2014 has become significant enough to merit the extension there of a major local bus service, which has given the 27 a more useful objective than had been the case ever since being pulled back from Richmond. Seen coming up to Notting Hill Gate on 4 May 2015 is Stamford Brook's ADH 26 (YX62 FDY).**
Matthew Wharmby

Both ADHs 1 and 2 had been refurbished by April 2015; meanwhile ADH 14 exchanged its Lord Mayor's Appeal ad for one extolling the dubious virtues of Crocs footwear. In June this latter was given an ad for *Shrek* and ADH 5 received one for Sunglass Hut; ADH 11 had regained red by this time.

Park Royal's ADH 46 suffered frontal damage on 18 July at Hammersmith when hit by a police car en route to a call; it was back in service on 6 August. On 31 July Shepherd's Bush's ADH 27 incurred more severe damage by hitting a lorry in Kensington High Street while on the 27. In July ADH 16 exchanged its

Above: **Accident damage to Epsom Buses' DD 15 on 31 March prompted a plea for help to fellow RATP company London United, which supplied ADE 45 (YX62 BZS) to assist on the 406 and 418. Here it is having arrived at Kingston at 6.50 pm on 17 April as a 406, but due to the complex nature of cross-linking between the two Epsom Buses routes, about to leave as a 418.** *Matthew Wharmby*

Left: **Little has affected the ADE and ADH classes of London United since their delivery, but those ADHs based on the 94 undergo the application and rotation of overall advertising liveries with great rapidity. Seen on ADH 6 (SN60 BYA) in Oxford Street on 9 November 2015 is one of TfL's own in-house ads, this one extolling the green virtues of hybrid technology.** *Matthew Wharmby*

Right: **Another Shepherd's Bush E40H with an ad livery was part of the big push to bring tourists to the Philippines during 2015; this particular version was for Albay and was carried by ADH 8 (SN60 BYC), seen in Oxford Street on 9 November 2015.** *Matthew Wharmby*

Below: **It's been three years now since London United bought its last Enviro400s of either diesel or hybrid format; a comparatively fallow period for the company has seen only an additional contingent of Volvo B5LHs enter service, and it remains to be seen whether any more E40Ds or E40Hs will appear in 2016. For the moment here is one of the 27's regular buses out of Stamford Brook, ADH 27 (YX62 FFB), seen in full winter sunshine on 16 January 2016 at Warren Street.** *Matthew Wharmby*

Peru ad for one promoting Walls ice cream, and in August ADHs 5 and 46 lost their ads (Sunglass Hut and Kathmandu respectively) for red. In September ADH 6 was treated to a Green Bus ad scheme.

In October five ADHs underwent changes to their ads; ADH 14 resumed red, ADH 15 gained a scheme for Hungry House, ADH 16 exchanged its Walls ad for one for Mexico (a scheme also gained by ADH 22) and ADH 21 took on a scheme for Karen Millen. In November ADH 11 received an ad for Campo Viejo and at the end of 2015 ADHs 16 and 22 were returned to red (ex-Mexico). January 2016 saw all of ADHs 4, 8, 11, 12, 15 and 21 lose their advert liveries for red.

Registrations

ADH 1, 2	SN58 EOR/S
ADH 3-22	SN60 BXX-Z, BYA-D/F-H/J-M/O/P/R-U
ADH 23-51	YX62 FAU, FCM, FDD/Y, FFB/G, FHA/O, FJD, FJV, FKE/K, FLH, FME/G/V, FNZ, FOA, FPC/F/K, FSE/S, FTD/F/P/Z, FUT/U
ADE 1-23	YX12 FNG/H/J-P/R-Z, FOA/C/D/F/H/J, FON/P/
ADE 24, 25	YX62 AEW, AGU
ADE 26-32	YX12 GHJ/K/N/O/U
ADE 33-35	YX62 AHE, AOE, ARZ
ADE 36-45	YX62 BXF/U/R/Y/Z, BYG/J/K, BZE/S
ADE 46-73	YX62 BBO/Z, BCK/V, BFL/U, BGE/F, BHD/W, BJF/U/Z, BKF/O, BLZ, BMV/Y, BNO/V, BPF/O/U/Z, BUA/E, BVN, BWO

Date	Deliveries	Licensed for Service
01.09	ADH 1, 2	ADH 1, 2 (**HH**)
10.10	ADH 3-16	
11.10	ADH 17-22	ADH 3-22 (**S**)
06.12	ADE 1-10	ADE 1-10 (**AV**)
07.12	ADE 11-23, 26, 27	ADE 11-23, 26, 27 (**S**)
08.12	ADE 24, 25, 28-38	ADE 28, 29 (**S**)
		ADE 30-32 (**AV**)
09.12	ADE 39-45, 46-51, 53-62	ADE 24, 25, 33-45 (**AV**)
10.12	ADE 52, 63-73	ADE 46-48, 51, 53-58 (**S**)
		ADE 49, 50, 52, 59-73 (**PK**)
01.13	ADH 23-32	ADH 23-32 (**V**)
02.13	ADH 33-47	ADH 33-47 (**V**)
03.13	ADH 48-51	ADH 48-51 (**V**)

Above: **The restoration of Sovereign to partnership with London United brought with it the former's taste for Volvo B5LHs, and no further orders for Enviro400s seem likely at the time of writing. To sum up examples of both varieties as of 2016 are Park Royal's ADE 58 (YX62 BJZ) passing Shepherd's Bush's ADE 4 (SN60 BXY) at Shepherd's Bush Green on 21 Febrary 2016.**
Matthew Wharmby

Quality Line

DD 1-18

In its long existence on the borders of Surrey and Greater London, Epsom Coaches had built up a reputation for reliability and quality coaching operations, exemplified by their distinctive and attractive coaches in their cream and maroon livery with prancing racehorse decal.

Since deregulation the company had diversified into the local bus sector, creating an offshoot known as Epsom Buses and operating a host of local routes with minibuses. Along the way the trading name was changed to Quality Line. Ultimately, it took a foothold in tendered London bus operations and achieved stability in this role. But the major coup for Epsom Buses was the winning of two double-deck routes, its first, in October 2006. These were the 406 and 418, heading south-west from Kingston to Epsom; the one on the main road and the other diverting via Stoneleigh on its way. Although much curtailed since their Country Area and London Country heyday, the routes had stabilised after some years of troubled and inconsistent operation by Arriva Croydon & North Surrey, the last incarnation of the successor to LCBS in this part of the world. This had been achieved by bringing them

Below: **DD 10 (SK07 DZL) was the highest-numbered of Epsom Buses' brand new Enviro400s taken for the 406 and 418 from 30 June 2007, trading as Quality Line. It is seen taking on passengers in Eden Street, Kingston, on the first day of operations.**
Matthew Wharmby

into the TfL network and allocating them to London United; by 2006 the 406 was operated with Volvo Olympians and the 418 Dennis Dart SLFs. The PVR on each route was four buses daily, and together, with a spare for each, that made a viable order for a proposed May start.

Ten Alexander Dennis Enviro400s were ordered, and on 15 and 16 January 2007 the company borrowed ED 3 from Travel London to test up and down the 406 and 418 roads. At the same time the assumption date of the routes was set as 30 June.

Classified DD 01-10 and displaying the leading zero on their body sides, the first of the new buses was delivered on 23 May. They were to 10.1m H41/26D specification and were registered with Edinburgh marks by the manufacturers.

And that was about it, the operation settling down very quickly with next to nothing to trouble either route. Occasionally the 406 and 418 would see visits by examples of the company's other available vehicles, namely the 293's Citaros and various types of short Darts and Enviro200s, and a little later Optare Versas. Conversely, when the X26 was taken over from Metrobus its first day saw a double-decker (and the loadings certainly warranted it!).

It took till October before adverts started appearing on the side of the DDs; while handsome in their all-red, the buses lacked advert frames and the ads were thus applied directly to the bodywork.

One measure of success for the company was the winning of the *Route One* magazine awards for the best medium-sized (31-100 vehicles) operator of the year. A timetable change from 29 March 2008 added a little more running time on the same frequencies.

While the 293 was still operated by Epsom Buses, DDs were apt to appear on it, with the 293's Citaros returning the favour, but the route passed to Metrobus on 30 August. DDs were also known to pitch in on rail replacements, despite there being no reduction in their routes' PVR at weekends.

The Epsom garage won Bus Garage of the Year at the UK Bus Awards ceremony on 12 November 2009, while the following year's competition saw the company as a whole take runner-up for best independent operator.

Another low-PVR route to merit double-deckers was the 467, which Epsom Buses won from London United in December 2010 for a 3 September 2011 start. It needed two buses, and two more Enviro400s were ordered. These were DDs 11 and 12, this time to H41/24D capacity. In July the 406 was retained for five more years with the existing buses and the 418 given a two-year extension on its current contract; these terms would apply from 30 June 2012.

DDs 11 and 12 arrived on 5 July 2011, two months before they were needed, and were added to the 406 and 418's complement when taxed on 1 August. They carried in-house advertising for the Epsom Coaches operation. In October another Enviro400 was ordered as spares margins were tight; this would be delivered on 2 February 2012 as DD 13, unusually with a Beverley registration. In the interim a design change had brought in the

E40D designation, which this was, with the accompanying frontal revision to bumpers and light clusters. As well as bolstering numbers, it helped cover for the first Enviro400s going away for refurbishment, one of the terms of the contract for the 406 and 418. This process began in late February, DD 01 being done over March and returned on 2 April. DD 09 was moved up in the queue by virtue of its de-roofing under the bridge at Hook Road in Epsom on 22 March.

On 14 April 2012 the X26 was taken over from Metrobus, and once again the Mercedes-Benz Citaro was chosen as the full-size single-deck allocation. These were joined occasionally by existing DDs; for the moment, only DD 13 had blinds for the X26.

On 19 April the company was purchased by RATP Dev, the last two members of the founding Richmond family having retired. No moves were made to unite operations with neighbouring fellow RATP company London United, but the paint shop at Epsom was quickly allotted some London United vehicles to repaint. An 'Epsom Coaches Group' logo began to appear from around this time, first seen on DD 01. After a year's lull, all refurbishments to the first ten DDs

Above: **On a sunny 27 May 2012 morning, DD 13 (YX61 FYR) arrives at Kingston after a journey on the 406.** *Matthew Wharmby*

were done by mid-2014. In the process they lost two seats, becoming H41/24D like their newer counterparts.

The 411 was added to the list of DD possibilities when the double-decks started turning up on this otherwise Versa-operated route from December 2012. In May 2013 DD 01 was named *Ricky Cliff*.

In November 2013 the 418 was retained on tender, with a jump in PVR from four to seven buses announced to accompany this from 28 June 2014. An order was placed in February for five more E40Ds, which arrived between 10 and 13 June as DDs 14-18; these

were the first TfL buses to Euro 6 emissions specification, producing a longer length (and greater weight) than hitherto. They entered service between 22-25 June, in time for the formal contract adoption on the 28th.

As well as the boost to the 418, the 406 was also increased in frequency during the daytime from two to three buses an hour on 28 June. Additionally, the schedules for both were formally combined under one running number series.

Accident damage to DD 15 sustained on 31 March prompted the loan from London United of similar E40D ADE 45 till 27 August.

Left: **DD 13 (YX61 FYR) is seen again, but this time it's adding capacity to an X26 journey on 15 April 2012, just a day after the route was won from Metrobus. As the only orbital route and providing a vital and unique link from southern suburbs to Heathrow Airport, the X26 has not only been crying out for larger buses but to be joined by additional orbital routes, as promised in the Mayor's manifesto. Neither arrived.** *Matthew Wharmby*

Above: **For all its short length, the 411 is the only TfL carrier away from Kingston to the west, and it's invariably packed with passengers not wishing to pay the Surrey premium on parallel TGM/Travel London/ Abellio services. Therefore, it was foolish to convert it to single-deck operation in 2005, a decision that has never been remedied, but at least DD 09 (SK07 DZJ) is making the effort when spied at Hampton Court on 12 November 2013.**
Matthew Wharmby

Right: **Looking clean despite filthy weather in Kingston town centre on 29 October 2014 is DD 16 (SL14 LNF) of this year's expansion batch. White-on-black blinds had come in since the previous set of Quality Line E40D deliveries, and the fleetname is new too.**
Matthew Wharmby

Registrations

DD 01-10	SK07 DZA-H/J/L
DD 11, 12	SN11 BVG/H
DD 13	YX61 FYR
DD 14-18	SL14 LND-H

Date	Deliveries	Licensed for Service
05.07	DD 01, 06	
06.07	DD 02-05, 07-10	DD 01-10 (**EB**)
07.11	DD 11, 12	
08.11		DD 11, 12 (**EB**)
02.12	DD 13	DD 13 (**EB**)
06.14	DD 14-18	DD 14-18 (**EB**)

CT Plus

HEA 1

Hitherto ekeing out its main batch of 2003-vintage East Lancs-bodied Dennis Tridents with second-hand PDLs from London General, CT Plus took a single E40H in December 2012. Classified HEA 1, it was actually acquired on behalf of University College London for use in accessibility research combined with studying the effects of acceleration and deceleration on passengers. It went into service on the 388 on 25 February 2013.

Little ensued until 2015, when CT Plus won the 26 for 27 February 2016 takeup and ordered 21 more E40Hs, but this time to the new City spec and losing the class coding to be numbered 2501-2521 (implying the renumbering of HEA 1 as 2500). Until they arrive, E40Ds were hired from Tower Transit.

Registration
HEA 1   SN62 DND

Date	Delivery	Licensed
12.12	HEA 1	
02.13		HEA 1 (**HK**)

Hired from Tower Transit, 27.02.16:
DN 33629-33635, 33637, 33638, 33640, 33642-33650, 33652

Above right: **Indistinguishable from any Enviro400 of any other TfL contractor other than by interior decor and company fleetnames is HEA 1 (SN62 DND), seen at Shoreditch High Street on 6 January 2015.**
Matthew Wharmby

Right: **CT Plus's most significant gain so far is the 26, assumed on 27 February 2016 from Tower Transit and, until its regular new vehicles are delivered, operated by the previous incumbent Enviro400s on hire. Recognisable as a CT Plus vehicle only by the running number card in the windscreen (Tower Transit inherited First's annoying habit of not displaying them), DN 33629 (SN11 BNZ) is at Waterloo on 28 February.**
Matthew Wharmby

Stagecoach London

Stagecoach East London had the honour of taking into stock the second Enviro400 prototype, allocated as a replacement following the destruction by terrorist action of Trident 17758 on 7 July 2005. Numbered 18500 and registered LX55 HGC, the 10.8m vehicle, on a modified Trident chassis and seating 76 (H45/31D), was handed over at City Hall on 3 October and made a gala appearance at Coach & Bus on the 5th and 6th, alongside the single-door West Midlands-spec prototype.

18500 was different in another way in that it carried a name, *Spirit of London*, in a heartfelt gesture to boost Londoners' morale. It was intended for operation out of Stratford on the 30 and entered service as such. For the moment, it retained its orange LED blinds, which were not otherwise trusted by TfL.

The intention to re-register the vehicle R30 SOL, to match its name, was dropped due to that combination of letters invoking something quite different when spoken aloud (!) and it retained its booked LX55 HGC. Pre-service modifications were carried out at Dennis's premises in Guildford during November and Metroline, who had ordered Enviro400s early and would end up with the first big batch in London, looked it over when it visited Holloway garage on the 22nd.

Formally taken into stock on 30 December, 18500 finally entered service on the 30 on Wednesday 25 January 2007, the honour of taking it out for the first time after a small ceremony at Stratford garage going to George Pseradakis, who had been at the wheel of 17758 on 7/7. As well as the 30, *Spirit of London* was cleared for routes 26, 86, 158 and 257, but appearances away from the 30 were comparatively few. On Sunday 17 September, to accompany a running day on the heritage components of the 9 and 15, 18500 performed two round trips on the normal 15, operated since its OPO conversion by Bow.

The Enviro400 was now the only future choice for customers who had previously taken either the Plaxton President- or Alexander ALX400-bodied Trident; the last of the latter to Stagecoach were delivered for the 47 early in the summer and an order for ten more 10.8m Enviro400s was placed for the 61 at Selkent following its winning back from First. But the momentous sale of Stagecoach East London and Selkent to Macquarie on 23 June threatened to throw a spanner in the orderly scheme of vehicle acquisition and replacement, because the new owners would favour the cheaper, Polish-built Scania and no further E400s would be ordered until the equally jaw-dropping circumstance that returned Stagecoach East London and Selkent to the streets of London as if they'd never been away.

The new fleetnames were East London and Selkent, with the old pre-privatisation sailing barge and hops logos respectively, and they were accompanied by repaints to all-red; 18500 lost its blue skirt by September. As well as visiting the 15 from Bow, it also turned out on that garage's 277 and 8 once each; this was helped by it having LED blinds, which were obliged to be removed under TfL's policy prohibiting them despite their better versatility.

The 61's assumption date was 2 December 2007, and to prepare Bromley garage for its impending new intake, 18500 was transferred in on 17 October, staying put till 22 November to train drivers. The numbering for the 61's new motors was 19131-19140, continuing what Stagecoach had intended prior to being taken over but obviously throwing up future problems; to this end, the East London Bus Group (as was the name for the

overall holding company of East London and Selkent) were granted permission to use the asset numbering system for a year.

Only three of the new buses had been delivered by the time the 61 was taken over on 2 December, the route commencing with TAs and TASs transferred in ones and twos from elsewhere in the combined fleet. The first Enviro400s hit the street on 6 December and all ten were in service within a fortnight. It didn't take long for one to visit the 269, on 5 January 2007, and from February examples began visiting the 208. 19 April saw 19139 on the 638 school bus, and in May Surrey contract route 516 saw two E400s.

Spirit of London 18500, meanwhile, was fitted with old-fashioned roller blinds in time for the bus to appear at the Longcross incarnation of Cobham this year, and in November received a set of blinds including Bow's 8 and Leyton's 55 as well as its own Stratford routes. On 24 February 2008 Stratford closed and 18500 was transferred to the new West Ham; eight days earlier it had participated in an enthusiasts' tour of the garage sites that were set to be swallowed up by construction of the Olympic Park. Its move to West Ham brought in further

Above: **The first Cobham open day after the delivery of 18500 (LX55 HGC) saw *Spirit of London* displayed with its prominent fleetname and dedication to the population of the city it served. Attractive in an understated way, the Enviro400 in this form would eventually reach a strength of over two thousand.**
Matthew Wharmby

Left: **The same vehicle at the same event, although a year later and at the temporary Longcross site used only in 2007. The blue skirt has gone, East London fleetnames have been applied and the LED blinds have been replaced by unfortunately ill-fitting roller blinds which provide so little information as to be near-useless.** *Matthew Wharmby*

opportunities, and during April and May it performed regularly on the 257, 26 and even once on the 241.

By April 2008 19131-19140 had been downseated from H45/31D to H45/30D by simply locking the tip-up seat opposite the wheelchair area, and in July 18500 followed suit.

2008 and 2009 proved stable for the eleven E400s in the fleet; iBus was duly fitted, and on 27 June 2009 the 26 and 30 were reallocated from West Ham to Bow, leaving the 257 as 18500's regular pitch. *Spirit of London* also saw use on the 115 and 277, two routes new to it. When the 69 was transferred to West Ham on 28 November, 18500 was out on the first day.

The year 2010 was characterised for the E400 fleet by absolutely nothing; nothing but the spectacular return to London of Stagecoach on 14 October. Immediately the old fleetnames began making their way back to buses' fronts and sides. There was not a lot of renumbering other than to the Enviro200s and Optare Versas and Tempos; indeed, two double-deckers that had taken the numbers 19131 and 19132 since the London companies had left now clashed, so were renumbered 19317 and 19318. *Spirit of London*, meanwhile, was renumbered from 18500 to 19000 to more properly identify it as the first of the Enviro400s rather than the last of the Tridents. A hiccup saw it physically numbered 18900 for a spell until correction.

Where ELBG had favoured the Polish Scania, Stagecoach remained a resolute supporter of Alexander Dennis, indeed having put money into the organisation to keep it afloat, and in December ordered 124 Enviro400s for a number of contracts gained at the end of 2010. These began arriving in mid-February, numbered from 19711 up, and were to 10.1m length and H41/26D capacity.

The first 68 were built on two production lines of 31 and 37 respectively, so were delivered out of numerical sequence. Of the order as a whole, 19711-19733 were destined for Rainham for the 174, 19734-19741 to North Street for the 496, 19742-19755 to Plumstead for the 99, 19756-19785 and 19794-19805 to Barking for the 145, 169, 387 and 687 retained from 26 March (plus one for the 62) and 19786-19793 to Rainham for the 287. After that would come 19806-19834 for the 53 at Plumstead, scheduled to begin a new contract there on 30 July.

Prepared at Catford, the 99's examples were put into service at Plumstead from 2 March, but only five were working by the end of the month, other examples in store awaiting iBus fitment being detailed to cover the Cheltenham race meeting between 14 and 18 March. 19711-19713 entered service on Rainham's 174 on the 31st, but it wasn't till May before that route was completed; similarly Plumstead's 99 was all present by April and Barking was commenced on the fifth of that month, early entrants being concentrated on the 145. One route they visited that otherwise wasn't scheduled for them was the 5, and 19000 at West Ham was still wandering, now adding the 106 to its list of achievements. Plumstead's E400s, meanwhile, were sighted on the 53 in stength long before that route's own batch appeared.

Top: **Plumstead's first Enviro400s were for the 99, exemplified by 19749 (LX11 BCK) at Bexleyheath on 4 August 2012.** *Matthew Wharmby*

Above: **Creeping round the back of Romford on its way to the station on 7 July 2013 is 19733 (LX11 AZW) from Rainham.** *Matthew Wharmby*

Left: **As the major route at Plumstead garage, the 53 not only was likely to see newer vehicles meant for the more local services but would indeed receive its own batch, services in central London being considered more important for the introduction of new buses. Thus is seen 19746 (LX11 BBZ) drawing up to Woolwich market on 30 July 2011.** *Matthew Wharmby*

Right: **Barking's large intake of Enviro400s during 2011 displaced Dennis Tridents to other work within Stagecoach London; here in Ilford town centre on 3 July 2011 is 19756 (LX11 BDF).** *Matthew Wharmby*

Right: **It's a beautiful sunny day on 7 July 2013 and a perfect theatre to display buses at their best; 19716 (LX11 AYY) out of Rainham is thus seen having called at Rainham Tesco.** *Matthew Wharmby*

Right: **The awkward hairpin taking buses away from where they are most needed in Barking town centre (which is once again used by buses, albeit just the EL1 and EL2 routes which were envisaged as trams) is the backdrop for Barking's 19762 (LX11 BEJ) on 25 March 2012.** *Matthew Wharmby*

North Street's 496 was converted from 'TAS' between 17-20 May, the new buses soon making appearances on the 103, 175, 247 and 294, and by the end of May the 287 out of Rainham was fully provisioned. Barking's batch were all delivered by 17 May, after which a pause ensued before the next batch. These arrived quickly from mid-June, a spot of excitement sending five to work from Bromley on Wimbledon tennis services alongside London General. Barking and Rainham were thus completed, the former being given the responsibility of preparing the buses for the latter.

Right: **19806 (LX11 BJO) and 19833 (LX11 BMV) are two of Plumstead's Enviro400s delivered for the 53, and on 16 October 2011 the one passes the other at County Hall.** *Matthew Wharmby*

Below: **Straying from the 53 to the 177 on 16 October 2011 is Plumstead's 19834 (LX11 BMY) in Woolwich.** *Matthew Wharmby*

July saw the delivery commence of the 53's new buses, albeit comparatively slowly until the factory resumed production in August after its annual two-week shutdown. They were mixed in operation with the 99's batch, of course. Over the river Barking's E400s now counted appearances on the 396, otherwise the province of E200s and/or Versas, and Rainham put out its new double-deckers in some strength on the 372. Confidence in the model was assured with a further order for twelve (19835-19846) placed for delivery by year's end; ten for the 199 (including school route 660) at Catford and one to supply a one-bus upcount on the 61. This route's existing buses were already coming due for a fresh coat of paint, 19135 being the first so treated in July 2011.

As they increased in number, Plumstead's E400s could now feel confident in wandering from the 53 and 99, racking up appearances on the 51, 96, 122, 177 and 472 while their Scanias or Tridents returned the favour.

It is worth noting that by this year Alexander Dennis had reconfigured the Enviro400 sufficient to merit a new pair of type designations; E40D for diesels and E40H for hybrids. Uniquely, Stagecoach insisted on keeping the original front light cluster, where everyone else had succumbed to the redesign which clumped them closer together so that a scrape, intended to carry five LED driving lights, could be added underneath. This would continue until the end of production of this body style, and was even the case with the new hybrids ordered by Stagecoach to take over the 15 from the 'TAs' that had ejected the route's RMLs in 2003. These were to be numbered 12128-12153, overwriting a block that had hitherto been the province of Routemasters. Numbering was to become an issue for Stagecoach Enviro400s, as the nineteen thousands were rapidly approaching their end and 19901-19999 were now reserved for oddments (such as the aforementioned Routemasters, a few of which were still in stock group-wide). Therefore, another order for E40Ds, placed in October for the 101 (Barking, recently acquired from the closed Upton Park), 275 (to be taken back by Leyton after two decades with Arriva and its Grey-Green antecedents) and West Ham (all the 238 and half the 104 and 158) would be numbered in the 10,000s, although some pencil-pushing had to be undertaken to firm up the blocks for them. Two further routes would need E40Ds in 2012; the 136 at Catford (whose contract-retention date was 26 May) and the 208 at Bromley from 1 September.

Built at Scarborough, 19835-19846 were delivered between 18-23 December and, while awaiting iBus fitment, were pressed into action on a gig taking athletes and officials to and from the Artistic Gymnastics at the O2 between 8-18 January; this was a test event for

the upcoming Olympics. Meanwhile, the 15's hybrids commenced delivery with 12128 on 15 December; this bus entered service on the 21st but no further vehicles entered service until January. To mark them out as hybrids, they carried a different interior with green sidewalls and floors, green-based moquette and yellow handrails. Catford's first E400s entered service on the 199 on 10 January; 19835 was deployed to Bromley.

There were now 79 E40Ds on order, and an amendment was made to fleetnumbering in that numbers would now proceed as far

Above: **Now numbered 19000,** *Spirit of London* **(LX55 HGC) is seen leaving Stratford bus station on 11 August 2012.** *Matthew Wharmby*

Below: **Plumstead's latest intake of Enviro400s would wander from the 53 more often as not, and the 177 on 14 April 2013 is the focus of this shot of 19832 (LX11 BMU), manoeuvring within Peckham bus station on its way out.** *Matthew Wharmby*

Right: **Now fully provisioned with double-deckers after an awkward spell with Dart SLFs that clearly couldn't cope, the 238 at West Ham could now take on new E40Ds like 19871 (LX12 DAO), seen on 7 July 2013 swinging into place at Stratford bus station for the first stop outbound to Barking.**
Matthew Wharmby

as 19871 and then resume at 10101; expected allocations were of 19847-19858 to Barking's 101 in March 2012, 19859-19871 to West Ham (part of the 104 and 158) in April, 10101-10112 to West Ham (route 238) in April, and in May would come 10113-10123 to Leyton's 275 (due to be taken over on 3 March and covered in the interim by existing Tridents), and 10124-10138 for Catford's 136. Finally, in July 10139-10154 would take over the 208 at Bromley.

The 15's conversion to hybrids was complete by February, and wanderings to the 8, 205 and 277 began during that month. Catford was not exempt, some of its new E40Ds making their way to the 47 to start with, followed by the 136, which of course was due new buses of its own.

This year's contingent of E40Ds started arriving in March, production again being split between Falkirk and Scarborough (which built 10124-10138). Prior to entering

Right: **The 15 is better associated with RMLs than anything else, having fielded the type for 37 years, but after seven years of OPO Tridents the route was now due something new, and these were E40H hybrids. The green-based seating is just about visible in this Charing Cross shot of Bow's 12134 (LX61 DFL) taken on the afternoon of 21 August 2014.**
Matthew Wharmby

Right: **The rear aspect of the E40H, complete with the various extra grilles for cooling and expulsion of cooled air from the upper deck. Seen opposite the Tower of London on 25 November 2012 is Bow's 12147 (LX61 DFC).** *Matthew Wharmby*

Middle: **There were just enough numbers left in the 19800s to incorporate a smaller order before numbers had to jump back by nine thousand. On 4 August 2012 West Ham's 19863 (LX12 CZS) arrives at Romford on the 158.** *Matthew Wharmby*

Bottom: **In the accepted order of things, each new bus carries a higher fleetnumber than the one that came before, but Stagecoach's all-numeric system didn't allow for orders to outpace the blocks allocated and thus had to overwrite previous assets. 10127 (LX12 DFA) is a Catford bus, and is seen at Lewisham on 25 March 2012.** *Matthew Wharmby*

service, 19847-19854 assisted on Stagecoach's Cheltenham races service between 13 and 16 March. 24 March saw the first of the 136's E40Ds put into traffic and on 6 April the 101 began following suit. This route was complete by the 24th, which was when West Ham's buses commenced; not only on their intended 104 and 158 but the gamut of routes there, comprising the 69, 97, 104, 106, 147, 158, 241 and 257! West Ham's next batch then arrived, dropping numbers back into the ten thousands and in practice mixed with those in the nineteen thousands.

Leyton's batch for the 275 commenced on 11 May and all of Stagecoach East London's allocation had been delivered by the 24th. Those for Selkent arrived during June and into July, the 208 seeing its first example on 30 June in the form of 10145. Most of this batch attended Silverstone on 7 July to serve as park and ride buses, and appearances away from the 208 soon ensued, the 269 starting the ball rolling. Bromley's incumbent 19131-19140 were undergoing routine repaints at the same time.

The craze of all-over vinyl ads was now ramped up in time for the Olympics, and in June 19721 and 19731 were treated to pieces for Vodafone.

To fulfil the conditions of the new contracts on routes 103 and 175 that specified a proportion of new buses, nine new E40Ds were ordered and these, numbered 10155-10163, were delivered during September.

suffered its own reverse as midnight struck on 19 October when two teenage passengers set fire to it as it arrived at Walthamstow Central on the 69. Extensive damage was done to the upper deck, but Stagecoach resolved to rebuild it at a cost of £50,000.

In January 2013 Stagecoach East London were awarded the 252 and 365 as part of a set of tendering victories that would contribute to the exit of FirstGroup from London altogether. When the 179 was added to this haul, an order for 19 E40Ds was placed for September delivery, which would furnish the 179 in its entirety and form a partial share on the latter with existing Scanias moved up from the 106 upon its loss to Arriva London North.

19000 was duly repaired and returned to London during April, retaining its special livery but now allocated to Leyton rather than West Ham; its home from 2 May was the 55.

Amid the new batch was 10164, a one-off for Bromley; like its fellows in this order, it was registered in Scotland by the manufacturers. Booked 13-registrations with Sidcup 'LX' prefixes had been voided as deliveries were not until after 1 September when the year identifier became '63'. At the same time, the 261 was won, representing a return to Bromley after 25 years with Metrobus, and merited an order for 10184-10195; a thirteenth bus was tacked on as an extra for Plumstead's 51. This year's Silverstone park and ride was

Unusually they bore Essex marks, bringing back for the moment a once commonplace feature of Stagecoach buses in London; since the change to the registration system on 1 September 2001 the group had registered everything for London at the Sidcup LVLO. Their service debut was on the 20th, and the buses soon recorded appearances on Dart-operated route 296.

Having served as the replacement for terrorist-destroyed 17758, *Spirit of London*

Right: **Back in action after its burning and now based at Leyton, 19000** *Spirit of London* **(LX55 HGC) stages through Hackney on 23 April 2014.** *Matthew Wharmby*

carried out by E40Ds from Leyton's route 275 allocation, their place being taken for the duration by 'TAs' displaced from the 230, which had also been lost to Arriva London North after its entire lifetime with Leyton.

Bromley's 10145 was loaned to Plumstead between 31 July and 3 August. Bromley's own 10164 was delivered on 10 August and entered service on 2 September. The two Vodafone-liveried E40Ds, 19721 and 19731, came due to have their ads removed in August after a year, but needed a repaint thereafter.

On 28 September the scene in Romford changed overnight, and was very different with no First now and Stagecoach very much in control. The 179, 252 and 365 were assumed with their intended buses (10165-10171 assisting Scanias on the 252 and 365 out of Rainham and 10172-10193 on the 179 from Leyton).

Right: **Stagecoach East London's new operations on the 252 were achieved by putting them into Rainham, whose 10166 (SN63 JVP) is seen in Romford on 6 October 2013.** *Matthew Wharmby*

Below: **Leyton had operated the 179 before, when a transfer from the closed Loughton was necessitated, and now came back with E40Ds like 10174 (SN63 JVZ), seen in Ilford on 2 September 2014.** *Matthew Wharmby*

Above: **The 261 was blue for four times as long as it was red, but on 21 August 2014 10191 (SN63 NBM) has restored Bromley to command.**
Matthew Wharmby

2013's representatives of a Stagecoach E40D were Leyton's 10182 and Plumstead's 10196, which received the treatment during October and kept it until November. 19748 received an ad for Stagecoach-owned Megabus in October and 19754 underwent a repaint after just two years! In November another Megabus ad was applied, but this time in a maroon colour to plug Megabus Gold for a month; the recipient was Leyton's 10179.

Events were now shifting the emphasis of London bus orders towards hybrids, and Stagecoach's fleet was about to double when an order for 57 (soon increased to 63) was placed alongside one for 32 Volvo B5LHs. The intent at first was to allocate the Volvos to the 54 and 75, which were won back by Selkent after five years under Metrobus, but plans would change repeatedly. Plumstead's 96, 122 and 472 had also been won, representing a retention on tender, and would be needing new buses. Ten more E40Hs were added, to cover the 372 at Rainham and add three buses to the 262 at West Ham; the batch would be numbered 12261-12333.

The 261's batch followed straight after, going into store at Bromley.

The Poppy Appeal had now become an annual fixture on London's buses, with a new design every year over a white base, and

On 18 November Bromley's new E40Ds began leaving storage and deploying, firstly to school routes 636, 637, 638 and 664 and then on the 30th to their rightful 261.

When the massive batch of E40Hs started arriving in February 2014, plans to allocate them were revised again and again. Eventually the output would be allocated to Catford for the 54 and 75, followed by the 205 at Bow and the remainder to Plumstead, where the Volvo B5LHs (numbered 13001+) would also congregate. In any case Scanias would be displaced to see off Tridents to the provinces, and as it turned out the Volvo order was reduced in favour of thirty more E40Hs, bringing the anticipated intake to 103 and all to the latest Euro 6 emissions specification. On 3 March 12261 was put into service on the 47 out of Catford, pending the formal takeover of the 54 and 75 on separate Saturdays. The E40Hs' use on the 47 constituted an official trial rather than just rogue appearances, as had been wanderings from the 136 and 199. Unrelated but relevant was a one-day swap on 19 March of the 47's Tridents to the 136 and 199, with E40Ds on the 47.

Catford's allocation was thus 12261-12292, with Plumstead to receive 12293-12303 and Bow 12304-12333, after which Plumstead would finish off the order with 12334-12363. Underscoring the almost sudden fall-off in corresponding orders for hybrids came an order for 10197, a single E40D to top up the 261 at Bromley.

Catford's E40Ds drifted into service over April after driver training was carried out, spreading out over the 47, 136 and their night counterparts. 12261 spent 19 April on loan to Bromley for a rounder on the 208, while 12262,

12263 and 1269 saw use at Plumstead on the 53 between 22 and 25 April. The 75 was taken over on 26 April and the 54 on 3 May, putting all the new buses into use on those routes. At the same time, the 13001+-numbered Volvo B5LHs were going into service at Plumstead and the 53, running as it did through central London, was selected for their main use alongside the 122, though a degree of mixing was natural. Once enough were in place, six E40Ds were intended to transfer to Rainham to form the 372's permanent complement.

2014 was TfL's Year of the Bus, showcasing the best in London's bus transport, and one of its aspects was the unveiling of heritage liveries. None was better than that worn by 10136 of Catford at Stagecoach Selkent, which was given not only a superb rendition of the Woolwich Corporation Tramways livery worn by L 136 in the early 1990s, but the M/T/L moquette of the Olympians' era. This bus was chosen specifically to recall previous ambassadors, L 136 and MD 136, and indeed was given the name the latter once held, *Selkent Ambassador*. 10136 made its debut at Brooklands on 13 April 2014, the repaint having been completed with only hours to spare, and was rostered thereafter on the 199. An accident on 11 May took it off the road until 11 June.

Lone diesel 10197, a Euro 6 model, arrived at the end of May but ended up being allocated to Catford. As planned, 19828-19833 were transferred from Plumstead to Rainham at the end of May and beginning of June.

In advance of the formal contract adoption date of 30 August 2014, the E40Hs designated for Bow were delivered from June and put into service as soon as they arrived; 12318 and 12328 were stragglers coming later.

The last diesel Enviro400s ordered by Stagecoach for London to the original design comprised 10198-10205, to cover the extension of the 136 from Peckham to the Elephant & Castle. This projection had already been set going with existing 'TASs' and helped the hard-pressed 343 on its unique section through the North Peckham estates.

19733 incurred some well-publicised damage on 21 July when it rolled away backwards from the 174's Harold Hill stand and crashed into a house. It was repaired by 16 October, but the damage to the house probably took longer to rectify...

Bow's 205 was completely E40H by 13 August, and Plumstead's thirty for the 122 and 472 began arriving in September, the first ten commencing by month's end until full takeover by 10 November.

September saw two new liveries, 10182 taking a six-month ad for Megabus and 10196 for Red Bull Culture Clash, a multiple-genre concert held at Earl's Court on 30 October. Once that was over, 10196 received an advert for Malaysia, while 10183 was one of this year's Poppy Appeal buses and 12144 was treated to a scheme for Relish broadband. In December 12131, 12133, 12137, 12140 and 12149 took ads for the addictive game Candy Crush Saga.

10198-10205 arrived from the first week of November and the first went into service from Catford on the 16th. However, a lone E40H, 12364, was added to Plumstead's fleet in February 2015. This was the last Enviro400 of the original design before the MMC development took over.

24 January 2015 saw three Bromley Enviro400s operating the 246 while their Enviro200s were needed to supply rail jobs, and this became a regular feature.

The conversion of 15 to Borismaster operation commenced on 2 March, its E40Hs transferring progressively to Leyton to take

Left: **The 205 has been the real success of the expansion pack of routes introduced in 2003 to accompany the Congestion Charge when it was only £5. Metroline gave way in time to Stagecoach East London and the Scanias it used were superseded in 2014 by new E40Hs like 12320 (SK14 CSY) seen at Bishopsgate on 2 September.** *Matthew Wharmby*

Below: **From RTs to RMs, Metropolitans, crew and OPO Titans, Olympians (both Leyland and Volvo) and then to Dennis Tridents, the 122 has ploughed on from Woolwich southwestwards to Lewisham, Sydenham and Crystal Palace. This year's buses were exemplified by Plumstead's 12354 (SN64 OHD), captured in Woolwich town centre on 3 December 2014. Stagecoach never was persuaded to adopt the new front.** *Matthew Wharmby*

up the 56. Once more dislodged from its employ when the 55 assumed LTs, *Spirit of London* 19000 had to transfer again, this time passing to Rainham for the 103 and 174.

10183 lost its Poppy Appeal ad in January, while all eight Candy Crush E40Hs at Stagecoach resumed red livery in February, as did 'Malaysia' 10196 and 'Relish' 12144, although 12142 received an ad for Green Bus, just in time to have to take it to the 56.

Although production had shifted to the MMC by 2015, one last standard-bodied E40H remained to be delivered; once more a one-off top-up, 12364 arrived in February and went into service from Plumstead on 27 March.

Above: **Eight new E40Ds were ordered to supply the 136's extension to the Elephant, and marked the last diesel Enviro400s Stagecoach would purchase. Seen setting off on its journey south from its new terminus on 12 April 2015 is 10199 (SL64 HYY).**
Matthew Wharmby

Left: **Blackwall DLR station on 17 March 2015 witnesses the transition on the 15 from E40Hs to Borismasters; already laying over is 12152 (LX61 DCZ), while LT 254 (LTZ 1254) nominally from the 8's batch at Bow, sweeps in to take its place.**
Matthew Wharmby

Above: **Displaced from the 15 by a Borismaster and sent to Leyton for the 56 is 12132 (LX61 DFJ), working through the Barbican on 4 May 2015. A Scania will have been the loser here, going off lease. Since their arrival at Leyton, E40Hs have made appearances on the LT-operated 55 as well as the 215 and 275.**
Matthew Wharmby

Right: **Positively the last original-body Enviro400 of either diesel or battery-hybrid format to be taken by Stagecoach London (and replacing two other contenders in that role during the compilation of this book!) is 12364 (SN15 LRJ), allocated new to Plumstead in February 2015 and caught in Woolwich on 10 September.**
Matthew Wharmby

A one-off ad was implemented on 5 June when 12137 out of Leyton was repainted bright green for World Environment Day; it did its piece on the 56 and then reverted to red. Its fellow hybrids on this route underwent a repaint programme during the summer.

Stagecoach East London took the 498 from Blue Triangle on tender with effect from 27 June, but its seven new E40D MMCs were not yet ready so Tridents were seconded to start it off. The new buses were numbered 10301-10307, and the first two made their debut on the Silverstone racing service before taking up on the 498 on 9 July (10301) and 10 July (10302); the rest followed by month's end. 10305 promptly had an accident on 15 July and was out of action for the next month.

Sadly, the period of glory for tramways-liveried 10136 came to an end on 19 September when it was repainted red and resumed service at Catford. In its eighteen months as a showbus the majority of its recorded appearances had been on the 136, with the 199 as runner-up and the 47 a distant third.

Stagecoach East London's route 69 was selected during 2015 as a testbed for another development of the Enviro400 in the form of the Enviro400VE (Virtual Electric), an electric version charged by induction plates in the ground at each terminus (in this case Canning Town and Walthamstow Central) so that the diesel engine backup only has to be used at all in an emergency. Four examples were ordered, later reduced to three on account of the budget running out, and were intended to go into traffic in November 2015. Part-funding comes from ZeEUS, a European undertaking which was also funding vehicles to be used in Bristol. But, as the vehicles finally began construction, the tender for the 69 was announced and Stagecoach lost it; thus the vehicles entered service as Tower Transit DHs.

12321 was given an all-over ad for Green Bus in September 2015 and 10196 was one of this year's Stagecoach entrants in Poppy Bus colours.

Moves of North Street's Enviro400s to Rainham and back during the spring of 2015 reduced numbers at the former until October when 19734-19741 came back to form the 496's permanent complement.

As 2015 came to a close, Stagecoach placed further large orders for Enviro400MMC-based vehicles; as well as the now familiar Volvo B5LH chassis, the integral MMC was also represented in both diesel and hybrid form. In 2016 we would thus see forty new

Left: **Barking's Enviro400 fleet is set to grow during 2016, but its existing examples are still known to turn out on the 5; here at Canning Town on 18 February is 19756 (LX11 BDF) doing so ahead of a more normal inhabitant of that busy route.** *Matthew Wharmby*

Below: **One of West Ham's regular runout is 10104 (LX12 DBV), seen departing Stratford bus station on the 238 during the afternoon of 18 February 2016.** *Matthew Wharmby*

Above: **The 205's hybrids at Bow wander fairly rarely from that route, but here at Highbury Corner on 18 June 2015 is 12312 (SN14 TYK). This is a comparatively recent terminus for the 277, which from its introduction as a tram-replacement service until 1990 penetrated further into town, but in 2016 it will have to be pulled back still further, to Dalston Junction, when rebuilding decimates this busy roundabout, turning it into a three-cornered affair which won't have the space to admit a bus stand.** *Matthew Wharmby*

Registrations

18500	LX55 HGC
19131-19140	LX56 EAF/G/J/K/M/O/P/W/Y, EBA
19711-19834	LX11 AYS-W/Y/Z, AZA-D/F/G/J/L/N/O/P/R/T-V/W/Z, BAA/O/U/V, BBE/F/J/K/N/O/V/Z, BCE/F/K/O/U/V/Y/Z, BDE/F/O/U/V/Y/Z, BEJ/O/U/Y, BFA/F/J-P/U/V/Y/Z, BGE/F/K/O/U/V/Y/Z, BHA/D-F/J-L/N-P/U-Z, BJE/F/J/K/O/U/V/Y/Z, BKA/D-G/J-L/N/O/U/V/Y/Z, BLF/J/K/N/V/Z, BMO/U/V/Y
19835-19846	LX61 DDE/F/J/K, DAA/O/U, DBO/U/V/Y/Z
19847-19871	LX12 CZA-H/J-P/R-Z, DAA/O
10101-10154	LX12 DAU, DBO/U/V/Y/Z, DCE/F/O/U/V/Y/Z, DDA/E/F/J-L/N/O/U/V/Y/Z, DEU, DFA/C-G/J-L/N-P/U/V/Y/Z, DGE/F/O/U/V/Y/Z, DHA/C-F
10155-10163	EU62 AXT/V, AYB/E, AZA/O, AAE/O, ADZ
10164-10183	SN63 JVM/O/P/R/T-Z, JWA/C-G/J-L
10184-10196	SN63 NBD-G/J-M/O/X/Y/Z, NCA
10197	SL14 DDE
10198-10205	SL64 HYX-Z, HZA-E
10301-10307	YY15 OYS-V
12128-12153	LX61 DFD-G/J-L/N-P, DDL/N/O/U/V/Y/Z, DEU, DFA/C, DCO/U/V/Y/Z, DDA
12261-12333	SN14 TVW-Z, TWA/C-G/J-M/P/U-Z, TXA-H/J-M/O/P/R-Z, TYA-D/F-H/K/O/P/S-V, SK14 CSX-Z, CTE/U, SL14 LRO, LNP/R/T-Z
12334-12363	SN64 OGG/H/J-M/O/P/R-Z, OHA-H/J-L/O/P
12364	SN15 LRJ

Date	Deliveries	Licensed for Service
11.05	18500	
01.06		18500 (**SD**)
12.06	19131-19140	19131-19140 (**TB**)
02.11	19711-19718, 19742-19751	
03.11	19719-19732, 19752-19760, 19762-19765	19711-19732 (**RM**), 19742-19746 (**PD**)
04.11	19733-19741, 19761, 19766-19778	19733 (**RM**), 19747-19755 (**PD**), 19756-19772 (**BK**)
05.11		19734-19741 (**NS**), 19773-19778 (**BK**)
06.11	19779-19805	
07.11	19806-19812	19779-19785, 19794-19805 (**BK**), 19786-19793 (**RM**), 19806-19812 (**PD**)
08.11	19813-19834	19813-19834 (**PD**)
12.11	19835-19846, 12128-12133	19836-19846 (**TL**), 12128-12133 (**BW**)
01.12	12134-12140, 12142, 12143	19835 (**TB**), 12134-12140, 12142, 12143 (**BW**)
02.12	12141, 12144-12153	12141, 12144-12153 (**BW**)
03.12	19847-19865, 19867, 19868, 19870, 10124-10138	10124-10138 (**TL**)
04.12	19866, 19869, 19871, 10101-10115	19847-19858 (**BK**), 10101-10112, 19859-19871 (**WH**)
05.12	10116-10123	10113-10123 (**T**)
06.12	10139-10148	10145, 10146 (**TB**)
07.12	10149-10154	10139-10144, 10147-10154 (**TB**)
09.12	10155-10160	10155-10160 (**NS**)
10.12	10161-10163	10161-10163 (**NS**)
08.13	10164-10181	10164 (**TB**)
09.13	10182, 10183	10165-10171 (**RM**), 10172-10183 (**T**)
10.13	10184-10196	10196 (**PD**)
11.13		10184-10196 (**TB**)
02.14	12261, 12262	12261, 12262 (**TL**)
03.14	12263, 12264, 12266, 12268	12266, 12268 (**TL**)
04.14	12265, 12267, 12269-12292	12263-12265, 12267, 12269, 12270-12291 (**TL**)
05.14	12293-12299	12292 (**TL**), 12293-12299 (**PD**)
06.14	10197, 12300-12317, 12319-12321	10197 (**TL**), 12300-12303 (**PD**), 12304-12317 (**BW**)
06.14	12322, 12323	12319-12323 (**BW**)
07.14	12324-12327	12324-12327 (**BW**)
08.14	12318, 12328-12333	12318, 12328-12333 (**BW**)
09.14	12334-12349	12344-12343 (**PD**)
10.14	12350-12363	12344-12363 (**PD**)
11.14	10198-10203	10198-10203 (**TL**)
12.14	10204, 10205	10204, 10205 (**TL**)
02.15	12364	12364 (**PD**)
06.15	10301-10304	
07.15	10305-10307	10301-10307 (**NS**)

First London

DN and DNH classes

After a very fallow spell in which no new vehicles were purchased in two years, First Capital found itself awarded the 498 in May 2007. This route was an unremarkable foray beyond the Essex borders hitherto operated by Arriva at Grays, but was to be extended further into the capital (specifically, Dagenham) and added two double-deckers to supplement five new single-deckers. Accordingly, six new Enviro200s and two Enviro400s were ordered for delivery in time to furnish a projected January 2008 start. Five more of the double-decks were added in August when First was

awarded the contract for route ELW, one of the replacement bus services intended to stand in from 23 December while the East London Line was reconfigured as London Overground. This order was subsequently boosted by one even though the sextet were not expected until into the New Year, and at the same time the 191 and 231 were awarded (the former as a retention and the latter operated at the moment by Metroline); 41 more Enviro400s were ordered for these and other projects as yet unannounced.

DNs 33501 and 33502 were delivered in December 2007, but as it happened the 498's

Below: **Braving the elements at the freezing 6 April 2008 edition of Cobham bus rally is Dagenham's DN 33502 (LK57 EJO), blinded for Essex local route 265.**
Matthew Wharmby

takeover was postponed from 26 January until June so the two could form the basis for the ELW, assisted by four TNs loaned from Westbourne Park to Dagenham.

The next intake of Enviro400s comprised DNs 33503-33519, which arrived in April and May and introduced powered smartblinds manufactured by Mobitec. Instead of going onto the ELW, DNs 33503-33508 were allocated to Northumberland Park as they arrived between 16 and 27 May so that they could be in place for the 231's assumption on 7 June. DNs 33509-33519 formed a mid-contract top-up on the 23 out of Westbourne Park. This batch introduced a slightly revised FirstGroup seat pattern which, unlike the last one, was properly symmetrical. DN 33501 was loaned from Dagenham to Northumberland Park to type train its drivers but was kept and put into service on the 231. When DNs 33521-33526, the 231's rightful allocation, arrived in June, DNs 33503-33508 were transferred to Dagenham where they were intended to form a temporary allocation on the D6 while its own DMLs transferred to Alperton to take over the 245, but in the event they were put into action on the ELW (as intended) and the D6 received TNs. However, the intended conversion of the ELW on 19 July from DN to DMS due to poor loadings was pre-empted two weeks early by the move of all six DNs to the D6. While at Dagenham they spread their net almost at once to school routes 652 and 686, Essex County Council contract TC0002 and a little later, the 150. While the schools were off in August, the 498 didn't need its double-deckers, so DNs 33501 and 33502 were used on the 179.

Westbourne Park's DN 33518 was guest of honour in this year's Cart-Marking ceremony on 18 June at the Guildhall.

Summer 2008 brought tendering victories for First as routes 179, 252 and 365 were retained with the promise of new double-deckers; this was confirmed in August with an order for 31 more Enviro400s. The outstanding vehicles of the existing order, DNs 33527-33543, began coming south from Alexander Dennis in October and this time were registered by the manufacturers, with Edinburgh marks. They entered service on the 191 from the 13th and quickly mixed with the existing DNs on the 231. On the 16th,

Below: **On 24 May 2008 Westbourne Park's DN 33509 (LK08 FMA) heads along Oxford Street with an Arriva MA in hot pursuit.** *Matthew Wharmby*

Left: **The 217 and 231 have always worked operationally as a pair, sharing the load down the Great Cambridge Road, but the latest tenders kept the former with Metroline and gave First the 231. Enviro400s like Northumberland Park's DN 33539, seen setting off from Turnpike Lane on 20 July 2010, became the staple.** *Matthew Wharmby*

Right: **The 191 was the other Northumberland Park route to receive DNs, exemplified at Enfield Town on 3 July 2011 by DN 33536 (SN58 CEX).**
Matthew Wharmby

Right: **The large batch of Enviro400s sent new to Dagenham tried as best they could to get around the restrictions imposed on the display of information by stretching the text on their blind sets vertically so that at least something was visible and useful. On 14 August 2009 DN 33567 (SN58 CHG) calls at Romford station.**
Matthew Wharmby

Right: **Dagenham's DN 33560 (SN58 CGV) sets off from Ilford on 25 March 2012, evading the pedestrianised town centre round the back.**
Matthew Wharmby

the main Dagenham batch started entering service on the 179, 252 and 365 and all were in place by 10 December, DN 33574 being the last to enter service in January. A change was evident here in that the First logo was in off-white rather than yellow. Following the rather underwhelming spectacle at the end of the Beijing Olympics by which London introduced itself as the next host by driving into the Bird's Nest stadium a mocked-up Enviro400 that opened to reveal David Beckham, among others, DN 33556 was displayed at the NEC on 4-6 November mocking up this mock-up! One final strange working out of Dagenham as the main batch took over was to Dart-operated 165, once a double-deck route and indeed the last crew service operating from Hornchurch in 1973.

DN 33519 suffered extensive frontal damage on 5 January 2009 while on the 23; it crashed into a shop in Westbourne Grove. It was repaired and returned to service in June.

Further tendering victories for First saw the company keep hold of all the E-routes already operated out of Greenford, and in January thirty-seven more E400s were ordered to replace 02-registered TNs from the E1 and E3. Assembled during April, the new DNs began coming south but iBus fitment backlog held up their service debut until 22 May. It was a full month before more than six were in service, examples being stored at Alexander Dennis's facilities at Harlow and Guildford as well as at First's own Hayes garage, but even then their deployment dragged out into September.

From this year Northumberland Park's DNs were now able to wander to the 259 and 476, two routes also retained on tender and expecting new VN-class Volvo B9TLs. Finally the 341 completed the set at this garage.

Now that the new Volvo B9TL had met TfL's noise requirement, production shifted into high gear as London's traditional Volvo customers, including First, switched orders to the type at the expense of the Enviro400. Those into Northumberland Park were accompanied by the odd DN straying from the 191 and 231 to the 67, 341 (until 16 October) and 357, while Greenford's large intake spread their net to the 92, 105 and 282. In July DN 33543, released by a new VN into Northumberland Park, transferred to Greenford to release a TN to Uxbridge to form the U3's schoolday double-deck complement.

After an enormous intake of Volvo B9TLs, First plumped for the E400 again when it won the 26 and 30 from Stagecoach at the

end of 2010. Now, of course, the models were designated E40D for diesel and E40H for hybrid, with a subtle alteration to the front light clusters and bumpers, and in December 44 of the former were ordered as DNs 33612-33655.

The early part of 2011 was quiet for the DN class, but in April the DNs for the 26 and 30 started arriving, in plenty of time for the 25 June takeover date. They were constructed on two parallel lines (DNs 33612-33630 and 33631-33654), each batch arriving in tandem. They remained in store until 25 June, when not only were the 26 and 30 taken on, but the 25 returned to First with 65 new VNs replacing artics; naturally the new DNs would wander to that route with Volvo appearances in payment. The new E40Ds were also apt to turn out on some of Lea Interchange's other routes like the 58 and RV1.

The 23 was awarded another five-year term with First and this time a mixture of Enviro400s were ordered for it in the form of twelve E40Ds and twelve E40Hs for delivery half in April 2012 and half in September. However, underscoring the increasing viability of the hybrid in the planning and purchasing operations of London's bus companies, this order was amended by year's end to 34 E40Hs. In any case further new VNs would bed in on the route first before moving to the 266, and when that was done, the existing DNs on the 23 would undergo refurbishment and transfer to the 607 in concert with VNWs displaced recently from the 150. At the turn of 2012 twenty more E40Ds were ordered for the 92.

In December DN 33543 returned to Dagenham and was replaced at Greenford by DN 33503. February saw DN 33511 put into Uxbridge to commence type training in advance of the conversion of the 607 to mixed DN/VNW operation (ex-TNL).

In the manner of Stagecoach a few years earlier, FirstGroup now made ready to divest its London operations; not for the monetary opportunities Stagecoach had pursued, but simply because the group was short of working capital and needed to recoup some, fast. On 29 February 2012 First announced the sale of Northumberland Park, its operations and buses to Go-Ahead (which would incorporate them into London General) and this was put into effect on 28 March.

The 607's first DNs entered service on 7 March, the others quickly following. DN 33543 further moved to Northumberland Park to displace a VN to Alperton and make a clear block of DNs 33520-33543 for transfer to London General on 31 March, where they became ENs 18-24 and 1-17 in that order.

The 23's first hybrids began to arrive, numbered in the block DNH 39111-39132 though many of them were mislabelled as

plain DN. Enough DNHs were in service by 19 May to displace to Atlas Road the required number of VNs for the takeover of the 266 from Metroline on that day.

Pending delivery of DNs 33776-33787 to finish the 23 and DNs 33756-33775 for the 92, the intervening hundred fleetnumbers since the 26 and 30's fleet were occupied by new E40Ds allocated to First Games Transport for the duration of the Olympic Games; while most of the buses operating on event services to and from the Olympic Park were VNs, 83 of the 'DNs' concentrated in force on seven Park & Ride shuttles from the Windsor area to Eton Dorney, where water events were taking place. The other seventeen were based at Atlas Road to cover tennis matches being played at Wimbledon. Two-thirds of the 'DN' fleet remained in situ for the Paralympics two weeks later before heading off to their permanent deployments (Manchester for 91 of them).

Once the Olympics and Paralympics were over and the hubbub had died down, the 32 new E40Ds could be taken from store and placed in traffic, both batches entering service beginning on 26 September. DNs 33756-33775 were straight replacements for VNZs 32328-32347 on the 92 out of Greenford, and four of them were registered after 1 September and thus carried 62-plates. Simultaneously DNs 33776-33787 began entering service on the 23, releasing twelve VNs to take over the 295 in concert with nine new ones. All were in place by October, VNZs and TNs being the losers in this shuffle. At Westbourne Park, the new buses were apt to wander to the 295 and even take advantage of the pooled status with

Above left: **The 23 was backed up by diesel E40Ds like DN 33781 (SN12 AVX), seen at Trafalgar Square on 25 November 2012.** *Matthew Wharmby*

Left: **Westbourne Park's new VNs liked to wander; this shot of DN 33777 (SN12 AVT) on 22 December 2012 shows the E40D at Clapham Junction visiting the 295, otherwise the province of VNs.** *Matthew Wharmby*

Atlas Road to visit the 328. Uxbridge's route 607 DNs, meanwhile, were known to visit the 427 and U3.

2012 brought an explosion in the all-over ad craze, and the inaugural First DNs to receive such schemes were Lea Interchange DNs 33612 and 33655 in November as part of Apple's massive push to sell its iPod. They lasted two months before reverting to red.

What would prove to be the final new order for E40Ds for First London comprised ten for the 6 July 2014 takeup of the 425 from Docklands Buses; skipping a number used in the provinces, they were booked as DNs 33789-33798. They would enter service with whoever came next, as in the spring FirstGroup admitted defeat altogether in London and after sixteen years sold the operation altogether. Taking First London's place, therefore, on the capital's streets, were two undertakings; the buses and operations of Greenford, Hayes, Alperton, Uxbridge and Willesden Junction would pass to ComfortDelgro under a new Metroline West identity complementing the already geographically neighbouring Metroline operations. The second brought Australians back to the running of London's buses after Macquarie Bank's inauspicious spell, as the buyers of Atlas Road, Lea Interchange and Westbourne Park were Transit Holdings,

one of Australia's myriad independents. The takeover was set for 22 June and would divide the DN fleet further. All that would be left of First, therefore, was the Dagenham depot, rebuilt comprehensively but reduced to total unviability by the brutal tendering process that had already seen most of its routes hoovered up by Stagecoach; the rest would be turned over voluntarily. Finally, on 22 June Go-Ahead would be taking the 193, 368 and school services 646 and 648, the latter mentioned (plus the 265 and 498) needing three double-deckers and thereby splitting the DN fleet three ways.

In April DN 33776 was treated to an all-over ad for Royal Brunei Airlines, and over the turn of May and into June DNs 33789-33798 were delivered. And perhaps the final act by a First London bus was the deroofing of DN 33639 under Homerton railway bridge while on its way back to base from a journey on the 30 on 7 June.

After the big sell-off, 35 DNs remained at Dagenham (First Capital East) with the 179, 252 and 365, remnants of the once-mighty Capital Citybus and before that, Ensignbus. But this operation was wound up on 28 September, the three decker routes passing to Stagecoach East London and all the buses turned over to First's disposal pool. DN 33570 was the last bus back into the garage.

Right: **After the grand sell-off on 22 June 2013 there was only Dagenham, bringing First full circle to where Ensignbus had begun in 1986. At Chingford station on 7 September 2013 we see DN 33560 (SN58 CGV); after the loss of this route to Stagecoach East London it would pass to First Leicester.** *Matthew Wharmby*

Below: **Dagenham's DN 33553 (SN58 CFZ) operates through Romford town centre on 7 July 2013; the 252 would achieve its quarter-century with this operator and its antecedents, but no more than three days thereafter.** *Matthew Wharmby*

Registrations

DN 33501, 33502	LK57 EJN/O
DN 33503-33526	LK08 FNE, FLX, FKX-Z, FLA, FMA/O/P/U/V/X-Z, FNA/C/D, FLH/J/L-N/P/R
DN 33527-33574	SN58 CDY/Z, CEA/F/J/K/O/U/V/X/Y, CFA/D-G/J-M/O/P/U/V/X-Z, CGE-G/K/O/U/V/X-Z, CHC/D/F-H/J-L/O, ENR/T
DN 33575-33611	SN09 CDU/V/X-Z, CEA/F/J/K/O/U/V/X/Y, CFA/D-G/J-M/O/P/U/V/X-Z, CGE-G/K/O/U/V
DN 33612-33655	SN11 BMU/V/Y/Z, BNA/B/D-F/J-L/O/U/V/X-Z, BOF/H/J/U/V, BPE/F/K/O/U/V/X-Z, BRF/V/Z, BSO/U/V/X-Z, BTE/O/U
DN 33756-33773	SN12 EHD-H/J/K/P/R-W, SN62 AAF/K/O/V
DN 33774-33787	SN12 EGY/Z, AVR/T-Z, AWA/C, EHB/C
DN 33789-33798	SN13 CGY/Z, CHC/D/F-H/J-L
DNH 39111-39132	SN12 APY/Z, ARF/O/U/X/Z, ASO/U/V/X/Z, ATF/K/O/U/V/X-Z, AUA/C

Date	Deliveries	Licensed for Service
12.07	DN 33501, 33502	DN 33501, 33502 (**DM**)
04.08	DN 33509-33513, 33516	DN 33509-33513, 33516 (**X**)
05.08	DN 33503-33508, 33514, 33515, 33517-33519	DN 33503-33508 (**NP**), DN 33514, 33515, 33517-33519 (**X**)
06.08	DN 33520-33526	DN 33520 (**NP**), DN 33521-33526 (**DM**)
10.08	DN 33527-33555, 33557	DN 33527-33543 (**NP**), DN 33544-33553 (**DM**)
11.08	DN 33556, 33558-33563, 33566, 33570	DN 33554-33563 (**DM**)
12.08	DN 33564, 33565, 33567-33569, 33571-33574	DN 33564-33574 (**DM**)
04.09	DN 33575-33581	DN 33575, 33576 (**G**)
05.09	DN 33582-33604	DN 33582 (**G**)
06.09	DN 33605-33611	DN 33577-33581, 33584-33587, 33589, 33590, 33592, 33593 (**G**)
07.09		DN 33583, 33588, 33591, 33594-33600, 33603-33606, 33609, 33610 (**G**)
08.09		DN 33608, 33611 (**G**)
09.09		DN 33601, 33607 (**G**)
04.11	DN 33612, 33613, 33615, 33616, 33618-33620, 33631-33640	DN 33612, 33613, 33615, 33616, 33618-33620, 33631-33640 (**LI**)
05.11	DN 33614, 33617, 33621-33626, 33629, 33641-33647	DN 33614, 33617, 33621-33626, 33629, 33641-33647 (**LI**)
06.11	DN 33627, 33628, 33630, 33648-33655	DN 33627, 33628, 33630, 33648-33655 (**LI**)
04.12	DNH 39111-39119, 39121	
05.12	DNH 39120, 39122, 39123	DNH 39113, 39114, 39116-39119 (**X**)
06.12	DNH 39124-39132	DNH 39111, 39112, 39115, 39120-39132 (**X**)
09.12	DN 33756-33762, 33776-33783, 33785	DN 33756-33762 (**G**), 33776-33783, 33785 (**X**)
10.12	DN 33763-33775, 33784, 33786, 33787	DN 33763-33775 (**G**), 33784, 33785, 33787 (**X**)
06.13	DN 33789-33798	*Entered service with Tower Transit on 06.07.13*

Disposals

31.03.12	DN 33520-33543 to London General
22.06.13	DN 33612-33655, 33776-33787, 33789-33798, DNH 39111-39132 to Tower Transit
22.06.13	DN 33503, 33509-33519, 33575-33611, 33756-33775 to Metroline West
22.06.13	DN 33501, 33502, 33505 to Go-Ahead London
28.09.13	DN 33504, 33506-33508, 33544-33574 to First disposal pool

Tower Transit

DN, DNH and DH classes

On 22 June 2013 Tower Transit, a specially-convened new British subsidiary of Australian-based Transit Holdings, acquired about half of the former First London bus operations, garages and vehicles. Among them were 46 Alexander Dennis Enviro400s and E40Ds (DN class) and 22 hybrid E40Hs (DNHs), the latter being based at Westbourne Park for the 23 and backed up by DNs (which could find themselves on the 295 when needed). Lea Interchange, meanwhile, operated the 26 and 30 with DNs with the possibility of wandering to the 25, 58 and RV1. Route 425 was scheduled to be taken up on 6 July with nine DNs already delivered to First London, DNs 33789-33798.

A new logo was designed, surmounting a circular device rather reminiscent of a cricket ball (and, so as not to offend Australia's cricket-mad sensibilities, we'll refrain from passing comment on the legality of its seam!). First's fussy five-figure numbering system, complete with its class codes bolted on at the front, was retained in its existing form.

Stability has ensued, DN 33639 coming back from repair in September 2013 and ad liveries covering DNs 33776 and 33780 (the Poppy Appeal and straight after that, the Asus T-100). DN 33776 followed those with one for the Lord Mayor's Appeal while its counterpart resumed red livery, and in February DN 33778 was plugging Schuh footwear along the 23 road. In April DN

Below: **Ordered by First but put into service by Tower Transit, the 425's batch of E40Ds is represented at Stratford on 7 July 2013 by Lea Interchange's DN 33791 (SN13 CHC).** *Matthew Wharmby*

33781 was treated to an ad for the animated movie *Rio 2*. This lasted until June, in which month DN 33778 exchanged its Schuh ad for one for TfL's own iBus system. In July DN 33782 was liveried for Bulmers cider, and in September DNH 39119 for Rimmel cosmetics. October saw DNs 33778 and 33782 lose their existing ads for vinyls advertising Relish Broadband and the 2014 Poppy Appeal respectively. In November DN 33779 took on an ad for Candy Crush, DNs 33778, 33781 and 33782 following in December, and the final event of 2014 as far as Tower Transit's inherited DNs are concerned has been the appearance of the type as extras on the 308, otherwise E20D-operated but having already proved during the Olympic Games that it could enjoy double-deck augmentation. Two double-deckers were indeed formally added to the PVR on 11 April 2015.

The 23's DNHs were ideally placed to take sponsor messages to the maximum number of potential customers; in January 2015 the Philippine government launched a major tourism campaign and, among others, had their message applied to DNHs 39112-39116

inclusive. DNHs 39117, 39118 and 39120 were added in February, while DN 33781 swapped its Candy Crush ad for one for Pepsi Max and DNH 39127 gained one for Green Bus, TfL's environmental showcase. In April DNs 337778, 33779 and 33782 regained red and in May DN 33776 was given an ad for Crocs. In June DN 33654 donned a scheme for the Sony PS4 and DN 33781 swapped its Pepsi Max ad for one extolling Sunglass Hut, the same month in which DNH 39120 resumed red livery and DNH 39127 went from a Green Bus ad to a Sony PS4 one.

Other than advert changes, little has affected this fleet since Tower Transit's debut, though the 295 left the ranks of Enviro400 possibilities when it moved to Metroline West on 31 October 2015. A minor but not insignificant tendering win was that of the N97 from London United for 5 March 2016 takeup; DNHs coming off the daytime 23 from Westbourne Park will be used.

In September Tower Transit received the word that it had been awarded the 69 for takeup in 2016; its vehicles would be existing

DNs displaced from the 26 by an order for new Volvo B5LHs, but this also meant that the new ZeEUs hybrid-electric Enviro400s would be coming to this company instead, rather than to Stagecoach East London. Intended as 12901-12903, Tower Transit rechristened them DH 38501-38503 and the first was delivered on 22 October. DH 38501 made its service debut on 9 November 2015, but appearances were sporadic thereafter, teething problems both on board and with the charging pads conspiring to cut the regular scheduled journeys; the pad at Canning Town hadn't even been fitted by the time services commenced. DH 38502 was delivered on 25 November and paired with its partner for a photocall on 2 December, and DH 38503 arrived a day after that. DH 38502

Above and right: **Activity stirred at Tower Transit after a very quiet 2015, first with the award of two routes and next with the diversion to the company of the three Enviro400VE hybrid-electric buses. The author was lucky enough to bag DH 38501 (SN65 ZGO) on its first journey on 9 November, the only one of the three intended route 69 rounders it had been able to manage that day, and indeed for quite a bit, as teething problems made appearances on the road rare until the other two DHs arrived. Both offside and rear nearside views were taken at Walthamstow Central.**
Both: Matthew Wharmby

entered service on 16 December, while DH 38501 sustained a smashed windscreen but was soon back in action. DH 38503 entered service on 7 January 2016.

In October 2015 DNH 39130 gained an ad for Campo Viejo while DN 33654 and DNH 39127 resumed red. Mexico ads were applied to DNs 33776 and 33787 during November. During January 2016 DN 33779 gained an ad for Costa Rica, while DNHs 39112and 39114-39117 all went back into red.

Prior to the takeup of the 69, the DNs earmarked for it were intended to be put through refurbishment; the 25's VNs would be treated simultaneously. However, the 69's takeover date was brought forward by three months to 6 February 2016, obliging the hiring of Stagecoach's existing Tridents, though DNs appeared on the 69 from the outset and the N69 was scheduled for DNs. The loss of the 26, now scheduled for 27 February, would send its E40Ds with it on hire to the incoming CT Plus.

Above: **The rest of the 69 passed to Tower Transit on 6 February 2016; the main ingredient was the existing Stagecoach 'TAs' on hire, but Lea Interchange's DNs from both the 26/30 batch and the 425 batch were present from the start; here at Stratford on 18 February is one of the latter, DN 33781 (SN12 AVX).** *Matthew Wharmby*

Left: **Another wandering Enviro400 on 18 February 2016 was DN 33654 (SN11 BTO), also at Stratford but this time on the 25.** *Matthew Wharmby*

Registrations
DH 38501-38503   SN65 ZGO/P/R

Date	Deliveries		Licensed for Service
07.13			DN 33789-33798 (**LI**)
10.15	DH 38501		
11.15	DH 38502		DH 38501, 38502 (**LI**)
12.15	DH 38503		

Acquired
22.06.13   DN 33612-33655, 33776-33787, 33789-33798, DNH 39111-39132
                from First London

Metroline

TE and TEH classes

etroline was an early adopter of the Alexander Dennis Enviro400, and indeed was its launch customer with an order for 28 placed in June 2005 for delivery at the end of the year. Their order was placed in the interests of removing all step-entrance vehicles from the company, as was being done throughout TfL's stable of contractors, but on an indirect basis as these comprised AVs on the 4 from Holloway and LLWs from the 186 at Edgware. Eventually it was the 24 that was selected for the new TE class's operation, which would displace its 2002-vintage VPs elsewhere and thereby cascade out the AVs and LLWs.

In this year two major changes had accrued to Metroline's fleet; firstly was the consolidation of the numbering system into a single rolling series, to which end the TEs were numbered 665-692 rather than from 1 upwards. Second was the introduction of a pastel blue skirt to replace the dark blue that Ray Stenning's design firm had phased in post-privatisation. It was strikingly sickly and was vetoed by higher management comparatively quickly, the TEs and a simultaneous batch of DLD-class Dart SLFs being the only Metroline vehicles to carry this variation from new.

TE 665 was delivered on 20 December 2005 and after a route survey over the 24, was followed by the end of the year by four more. Service entry was on 3 January 2006 when TE 666 performed HT509 and TE 668 HT508. Delivery was complete by March, but not before three had to take new '06' marks in place of their booked 55-plates. Wandering commenced early, with the 17 just one of the many choices available at Holloway. The 4 and W7 soon followed and by June the 134 and C2 had seen TE appearances. On 7 September the 143 school bus saw TE 670 and the set was complete by year's end with routes 43 and 271.

In May 2006 twelve more TEs were ordered for November delivery. In the autumn it was determined that these buses, to be numbered TEs 712-723, would go into Holloway for the 134, freeing up more vehicles for cascade, specifically for a 50% increase on the 16. They duly arrived on time and went into service albeit broadly on the 24 with the others,

four being detached on their way for tests at Millbrook proving ground. They reverted to Metroline's original shade of blue for the skirt and looked rather better for it.

Route 204 had been a Metroline staple ever since its introduction as the top end of the unwieldy 226, and it was awarded in August back to its incumbent with the promise of new

double-deckers to replace its current VPLs. These were ordered in December as 15 TEs for April delivery and were to be numbered TE 724-738. As they began arriving at the end of March TE 683 was loaned to Edgware to train its drivers. Twenty more were then ordered for new route 332, to be introduced in October as part of a revamp of the 16/32/316 corridor.

Edgware's new TEs entered service from 10 April in advance of the official contract date on the 28th and all were in place by the 30th. Appearances on the 113 ensued, with that route ultimately to get its own TEs, plus the 107, 186, 240 and 606.

By the middle of 2007 the early TEs were having their pastel blue skirts repainted dark blue in lieu of full repaints. The 332's

batch comprised TEs 828-847, and began to arrive at Cricklewood in late September in time for the introduction of the route on 13 October. However, TEs 843-847 were diverted to Edgware and entered service there instead, and when the 24 was lost on 10 November TEs 712-722 joined them, effecting a conversion to TE of the 186. TEs 665-692 stayed at Holloway, theoretically for the 134

but in reality covering every route where needed. Cricklewood's new TEs, meanwhile, turned out on the 16 from their first day.

On 4 November TE 715 was deroofed at the low bridge over Prince of Wales Road in Kentish Town while running dead to garage off the 24's night service. It was the first Enviro400 decapitated in London, but would not be the last!

Left: **TEs 843-847 were allocated to Edgware, in a late move, to join expellees from the lost 24 in converting the 186 from VPL to TE operation. Sooner or later they'd turn out on the 107, 113 and 240 as well, and here at Golders Green on the last mentioned is TE 843 (LK57 AXY) on 21 October 2009.***Matthew Wharmby*

The year 2008 was distinguished by some tendering victories and orders for Enviro400s to cover them (if indirectly); two to be won in the first half of the year were the already-operated 460 and E2. Forty-two new Enviro400s were ordered in March, and a fillip here was that five of them would be to hybrid specification (numbered TEH 915-919) for use on the 16. Rather than convert the 297 and 460 to TE as planned, it was decided to allocate TEs 878-914 to the 16 alongside the TEHs for comparison purposes, and TE 878 went into service at Cricklewood to this end on 28 July following its delivery on the first of the month. After a lull caused by Alexander Dennis's factory summer holiday, deliveries resumed and the 16 had its full complement of TEs by October. Appearances on the 32, 139 and 189 ensued, plus one on the 316 for Carnival. Despite the 390 being operated by King's Cross, its VPLs were pooled with Holloway and inevitably a TE sneaked over.

Thirty-two more TEs were now ordered to cover the win of route 91 from First and the retention of route 263 from spring 2009.

The TEHs were a different kettle of fish. TEH 915 was registered by Alexander Dennis on 21 July with an Edinburgh mark so that it could be used on road testing. All-red with the characterful leaf logos, the five arrived on 3 December after an unregistered example was displayed at the NEC, and when they went into service, displaced TEs 909-914 to Holloway to serve as the vanguard for that garage's proportion of the impending TEs 920-951 to take over route 91 in 2009; the balance of this order would be for the 263 at Potters Bar.

Above: Like the 24, the 16 was one of those routes that kept on getting new double-deckers as a priority, whether or not their contracts specified them. The 297 and 460 thus had to wait for their share, which materialised later as not-quite-new SELs. On 28 September 2008 TE 889 (LK08 NVD) arrives at Victoria.
Matthew Wharmby

Right: The rear of the TEH-class Enviro400 hybrid was replete with extra grilles, as seen on TEH 919 (LK58 CPV) at Victoria on 24 March 2013.
Matthew Wharmby

Right: The cheerful green leaves motif of the early hybrids must have been expensive to order and a nightmare to physically apply, so it didn't last long, not unlike most of the best livery improvements to dreary all-red. Cricklewood's TEH 919 (LK58 CPV) battles through interminable construction on its way out of Victoria on 24 March 2013.
Matthew Wharmby

The TEHs entered service on the 16 from 17 December, all except TEH 915, which lingered at Guildford until sent to Cricklewood on 24 December. It duly hit the streets in January.

To prepare Potters Bar for its upcoming intake of TEs, Holloway loaned TE 913 and later TE 910, which was in turn replaced by TE 681 and finally TE 909. The batch commenced delivery from the end of January 2009 and differed by having a pair of three-LED driving light clusters in each front bumper, recalling the foglights long since banished from British buses. The contracts commenced on 7 February but until enough TEs were assembled at Holloway the 91 (and N91) was assumed with existing examples, TEs 903-907 coming over from Cricklewood to help. The first TE on the 263 out of Potters Bar was TE 942 on 12 February.

Transfers from the conversion of the 263 to TE released TPs to Cricklewood and further displaced thirteen of its recently-acquired TEs plus five of Holloway's to Perivale West to convert the 297. Holloway's share thus comprised TEs 909-914 and 920-934, Potters Bar fielded TEs 935-951 and Perivale West could put into action TEs 891-908. Strange visitors at Potters Bar took in routes 82, 84, 217, 242 and W8 and at Cricklewood, the 210.

An order was placed in January for seventeen Enviro400s for the double-decking of the E2 at Brentford. These were designated TEs 976-992, and they started arriving from 30 August to ease out the TPs.

Above: **Potters Bar's first TEs comprised seventeen for the 263, personified on 2 June 2013 by TE 939 (LK58 KHD) at Barnet.** *Matthew Wharmby*

Left: **One of Metroline's typical shuffles of bus types made available enough TEs to take over the 297 from its incumbent TPs, and on 27 September 2009 Perivale's TE 898 (LK08 NVO), transferred from Cricklewood, is seen approaching Ealing Broadway with its blinds already set for the return journey.** *Matthew Wharmby*

Above: **All-red was now inescapable, and the E2's batch of seventeen TEs had just the headlight and taillight surrounds in a different colour. On 21 October 2009 at Greenford, TE 992 (LK59 DZT) is arriving while TE 979 (LK59 DZC) is leaving.**
Matthew Wharmby

Despite holding out a long time, Metroline now succumbed to TfL's edict to delete any livery embellishments at all, and these TEs were the first in all-over red, though retaining the black-painted headlight surrounds (which would inevitably fall to the red paintbrush in due course). TEs 976-992 were late arriving and had to be re-registered with new 59-plates, and the delay in getting them fitted with iBus equipment dragged out their introduction and it wasn't until 25 October before they were all in place. Inevitably they visited the 237, though this route now had its own Volvo B9TLs on order for 2010, and less often the 190.

Amid financial strictures affecting Metroline as much as any TfL contractor during what came to be termed the Great Recession, two routes still merited new buses when retained on tender, and these were the 139 and 189 pair. Twenty-four new Enviro400s were put on order against these routes in February, though the makeup of their type and allocation, as always with Metroline, would be up in the air until the last minute. As the spring progressed, ten TEHs were added to the 24 TEs, followed by another eight TEs and ten TEHs against the recently awarded contract that kept the 210 under Metroline, though in practice only

the 16 and 139 would be earmarked for the hybrids; to this end, the night service on the 139 had been seeing a spate of TEHs from the 915-919 batch recently. There were now enough in place or on order to make feasible concentrating large numbers at one garage, to which end the second batch of VW-class Volvo B9TLs on order would now be taking up the E2 so as to displace TEs 976-992 to Cricklewood. This year's contingent would thus comprise TE 1073-1104 and TEH 1105-1114.

On 23 July TEs 1073-1075 arrived at Metroline's CELF facility, the receiving depot for all the company's new buses, as the first of a two-stage process; the balance would be delivered in the autumn.

From 28 August until 17 December operation of the 186 and its buses, TEs 712-726, was outstationed from Edgware to Cricklewood while work was undertaken at Edgware garage. September saw the first TEs leave Brentford as VWs arrived for the E2, and all had gone by the end of October when the main batch of TEs resumed delivery. These had two fewer seats to comply with the reality that due to people claiming for supposed injuries caused by tip-up seats, it was more cost-effective now to deprive passengers of those two seats altogether.

14 November heralded the entry into service of the 60-reg TE batch at Cricklewood, covering the 139, 189 and 210. All ten TEHs also arrived that month, TEH 1110 carrying a placard proclaiming it as the 100th hybrid built by Alexander Dennis, though introduction was not until January due to the need to train drivers and engineers on a new set of mechanical features considerably different from the earlier batch. Cascades resulting from the introduction of the TEs and TEHs allowed the withdrawal of the earliest TAs new in 2000, plus the return off lease of several 03-reg TPs. Additionally, six SELs into Perivale West released TEs 890-896 into Cricklewood during December.

Above: **Inevitably repainted into all-red is Edgware's TE 846 (LK57 AYB) holding down the 240 at Golders Green on 18 October 2010.** *Matthew Wharmby*

Left: **Transferred from Perivale West to Cricklewood and nicely bedded in on the 210 at Brent Cross on 28 July 2012 is TE 990 (LK59 DZP).** *Matthew Wharmby*

Finally the ten TEHs entered service between 11-21 January 2011. One stylistic design was removed in that the leaves did not return, rather a discreet 'hybrid' legend being carried, but one returned in the shape of a filled white roundel with 'BUSES' along the bar. In February 26 more TEHs were ordered for October delivery. Another batch of VWs ordered at the same time would this time see fit to eject the TEs from the 297 and thus concentrate still more of the type at Cricklewood. For the moment, the first of the present batch of VWs into Perivale West (where they were intended for the 105) allowed five TEs to be loaned to Holloway to top up shortages there between 20 June and 1 July. Before they left, TE 903 turned out on the 105 to cover for a VW suffering broken windows in the spate of rioting on 9 August.

Now numbered TEH 1217-1242, this batch of 26 Enviro400Hs was funded by government to facilitate the full conversion of routes 16, 139 and 189, and started arriving in October. Both the first eight and next eighteen were different again from the previous two batches and from each other, and accordingly, were tried out under test conditions on the 189 as well as the 139 under CELF auspices, with at least one side trip to school route 632. After a period in store, all entered service between 15 and 27 January 2012.

At the end of the year, among orders for other types, an order for 11 TEs was placed for the 32, plus the promise of 24 more TEHs for routes as yet unspecified, in the Metroline manner.

Left: **TEH 1221 (LK61 BJY) was put into service at Cricklewood in the second half of January 2012. On 25 May 2013 it is seen pulling up to the set of bus stops carved out of the approach to the Bullring roundabout at Waterloo.** *Matthew Wharmby*

Left: **The proportion of TEHs on the 189 increased upon the introduction of TEHs 1217-1242, easing some minds (and lungs!) in the Oxford Street area. On 30 November 2013 TEH 1232 (LK61 BKU) leaves Brent Cross.** *Matthew Wharmby*

Left: **The 16 could now count a full complement of TEHs, using a mix of buses from four separate batches. Turning on final approach to Victoria on 17 June 2012 is TEH 1239 (LK61 BLV).** *Matthew Wharmby*

In the middle of January 2012 TE 886 was loaned from Cricklewood to Perivale West so as to release a VW to Holloway for type training; a very large number was about to arrive this year. TE 882 arrived later and both were seen in use on the 297.

2012 saw all-over ads spread like wildfire, and TE 1103 was Metroline's first, advertising M&Ms till February 2012. TE 1081 was next,

spending from March until June in a livery exhorting people to visit Hangzhou in China. May saw TE 910 go into a scheme for Thailand tourism (lasting two months) and June saw a big push by Samsung for its Galaxy S3 phone, during which TEs 904, 932 and 1102-1104 were treated; TE 914 was added in July, and in August TEs 1076 and 1099 were given schemes for Vodafone.

The 32's TEs were now imminent, and numbered TE 1307-1317, they appeared in May. In advance of their deployment they were stored pending their participation in duties related to this summer's Olympics. As per Olympics rules on commercial entities, no fleetnames were carried. However, in the usual change of plan, refurbished TAs from the final batch of 05-registered ALX400s recently displaced from the 266 were chosen to take over this route, the new TEs displacing older examples from the 57- and 08-registered batches in the 800s to Edgware to formally convert both routes 107 and 240 from VPL to TE operation.

TEs 925, 978, 1078, 1081 and 1098 reverted to red livery in September but TE 1094 was treated to an advert for Hangzhou.

Above: **The TEs purchased for the 32 ended up rarely working on that route; they were more likely to be seen on the 210, as TE 1310 (LK12 AVT) is doing when heading downhill to Archway on 5 April 2014.** *Matthew Wharmby*

Left: **On 14 July 2013 Edgware's TE 881 (LK08 DXS) is pulling into Edgware bus station at the end of its journey from Barnet. The semi-rural nature of much of this route does not disguise its need for double-deckers.** *Matthew Wharmby*

Probably Metroline's two key routes in central London are the 82 and 113, and their latest contracts were retained with new vehicles. The 82 would be getting new TEs 1420-1447 in 2013, while TE 1448 and TEH 1449-1467 would be for Cricklewood's 189 alone, to displace older TEs to Edgware for the 113.

TEs 904, 914, 932 and 1102-1104 reverted to red in October, but a huge push by Apple saw, among many others, Metroline's TE 678, 684, 691, 940, 1081 and 1098 liveried in a choice of different colours, as was the iPod in real life. December saw TE 678 and 940 resume red livery and the rest in January, but TE 1098's Hangzhou advert was modified on 1 February 2013, replacing TE 1094.

The 82's TEs arrived starting in February and once commissioned at CELF went into service, all being in use by 27 April despite some hiccups with transfers that saw some wrong identities being carried for a while. The TEHs arrived from March and were stored pending problems encountered with a revised refuelling system. TE 1448 entered service at Cricklewood on 19 April. They were to be the last Enviro400s (or their modern variant E40D and E40H) with the original body style, as the new MMC was under development and in any case, the Borismaster revolution was well under way.

After the fuelling system was sorted out, the final batch of TEHs took over the 189 during May and into June, releasing earlier TEs (in the 900s) to Edgware to render its double-deck allocation wholly TE-operated and thus include the 113 as well as the 107 and 240 and the 186 already thus operated. Meanwhile, the TEs from the 712-722 batch were undergoing refurbishment.

But greater things were in store for Metroline and no mistake. FirstGroup's ongoing monetary difficulties had caused it to divest its London operations, firstly garage by garage and then, on 22 June 2013, the rest. Tower Transit of Australia and ComfortDelgro, Metroline's Singapore-based holding company, divided it up between them and this saw Metroline West, as the resulting western half was named, inherit 69 DN-class Enviro400s which it renumbered into its existing TE series. Three Enviro400-

operating garages were represented in the five acquired; TEs 1571-1582 were for the 607 from Uxbridge, TEs 1715-1751 worked out of Greenford on the E1 and E3 and finally TE 1981-2000 were based on Alperton's 92. A lot of work was done to apply fleetnumbers and fleetnames within a month of the takeover so that the public perceived no difference, and when refurbishment came along, Metroline-patterned seat cushions were fitted, which sat incongruously amid the purple theme chosen by First.

Right: **In 2013 Metroline increased substantially in size by taking First's holdings right on its own doorstep. Greenford's E1 and E3 thus fit in perfectly, personified at Ealing Broadway on 29 June 2013 by TE 1723 (SN09 CEK), formerly known as DN 33583.** *Matthew Wharmby*

Below: **The small fleet of First DNs holding down the 607 also became part of the TE class, like Uxbridge's TE 1577 (LK08 FMX) at Uxbridge on 2 September 2014; this was DN 33514.** *Matthew Wharmby*

Bottom: **TE 900 (LK58 CNE) was one transferred to Potters Bar for the 217 and is seen on 5 April 2014 at Turnpike Lane.** *Matthew Wharmby*

In June TE 1098 exchanged its Hangzhou ad for one for Lycamobile and TE 911 took one for *Despicable Me 2*. This lasted till July, as did the Vodafone pieces on TEs 1076 and 1099. In September TEs 929 and 980 received ads for Nike and TE 900 one for the Burj Khalifa in Dubai. 2103's Poppy Appeal Enviro400s were TEs 903 and 906; these lasted till November, other than TE 980 which held out till February 2014.

Refurbishments of TEs rocketed along in 2013, one side-effect being to diminish the blue-skirted livery still carried by a sizeable number of Metroline vehicles.

Metroline had inaugurated the LT-class New Bus for London (aka 'Borismaster') in service, but when it came time for Holloway to convert a second route in the form of the 390 on 7 December 2013, vehicle cascades resulted that saw its VPLs stay put and release a number of 08- and 58-reg TEs to Potters Bar for the 217 and W8.

Refurbishment to all TEs numbered below 1000 was now complete, and the Uxbridge examples for the 607 now followed them through the process during 2014. In March 2014 Metroline took the opportunity to purchase TEHs 915-919, which had hitherto been on lease.

Despite the massive increase in numbers with the acquisition of five First garages, tendering could still swing the pendulum in the other direction and on 31 May Metroline West lost the E1 and E3, the former to Abellio and the latter to London United. TEs 1715-1749 were delicensed, but not before four

Left: **The clockwork motif of TfL's in-house iBus adverts, applied in connection with the Year of the Bus festivities, was charming and fascinating, even if the application to Holloway's TE 920 (LK58 KFW) was over a superannuated livery. It is seen posing in Regent Street on 22 June on a momentous day when this entire thoroughfare was closed off and packed from end to end with buses.**
Matthew Wharmby

topped up the 92 and 282 still at Greenford while simultaneously providing assistance to the 427's VWs (known at First as VNs) at Hayes.

For TfL's Year of the Bus, TE 920 was given an ad for iBus by which the workings were 'exposed' as if clockwork. It was rallied in Regent Street on 22 June with 39 other London buses past and present.

The MMC was now here, and Metroline placed an order for sixteen E40Hs with this revised and revamped body to service the 332's new contract from the beginning of 2015; while just outside the scope of this book, they were to continue the numbering system as TEHs 2072-2087.

On 2-4 July the 297 was converted from VW to SEL operation, the displaced Volvos moving to Holloway to eject nine TEs to Cricklewood to stand in on the 112 for its first month back with Metroline pending the delivery of long-wheelbase E20Ds. In practice this role was performed by TAs from the 638-655 batch.

The TEs lost from the E1 and E3 were divided; TEs 1715-1730 remained in store

Left: **2014's Poppy Day buses were a bit on the reticent side, there being somewhat fewer poppies this time around, perhaps because the ceramic version was to be seen in hundreds of thousands in the Tower of London's moat instead. On 3 December Cricklewood's inaugural hybrid TEH 915 (SN08 AAO), now owned outright, lays over at Oxford Circus.**
Matthew Wharmby

while TEs 1731-1751 were tasked with converting the 282 from TPs (which First knew as TNs).

Repaints to the TE 878-914 batch were completed in mid-2014, while TE 914 received a Bulmers cider ad in July (lasting until November) and TE 665 took one for the Nokia Lumia 930 in August.

On 8 November the 34 was taken over by Metroline with operation from Potters Bar. In characteristic fashion, the VWH-class Volvo B5LH hybrids ordered were to be diverted to the 82 instead and TEs 1420-1447 deployed to the 34 instead, but for the moment existing Holloway TEs in the 900s would deputise, released to Potters Bar through the re-use of the mothballed Greenford TEs and the late entry into service of the 112's DELs. In the event the 34 enjoyed a mix of VWHs and TEs, but as soon as all the new Volvos were

in place, the TEs stayed put at Potters Bar, releasing TPs to disposal.

TE 1751 was treated to Burj Khalifa colours in October, while TEH 915 became a Poppy Appeal bus. In December TEs 665 and 920 lost their adverts (all-over for the former, rear only for the latter). Repaints to ex-First TEs were commenced at CELF by the end of 2014.

On 31 January Metroline took over the 125, destined for the rest of the VWHs already operating the 34 and also making use of TEs. On 21 March another route was acquired, this time the 482 ex-London United and made the responsibility of Metroline West at Greenford.

Above: **First DN 33592 was renumbered by Metroline as TE 1732 (SN09 CFF) and remained in place at Greenford, moving from the lost E-routes to the 282 in 2014. Here it is setting off from Ealing Hospital on 4 June 2015.** *Matthew Wharmby*

Ex-First TEs going through refurbishment were allocated for the purpose.

Ad changes as 2015 progressed were to TE 670, which in March gained an all-over scheme for Invesco, while TE 1751 lost its Burj Khalifa ad in the same month. TEH 915 finally lost its Poppy Appeal livery in favour of one for Green Bus, TfL's own showcase of its environmental achievements so far.

Metroline's MMC order finally arrived in February, though all surrendered their booked 64-registrations for 15-marks (and interestingly, still booked by the company rather than the manufacturers, ensuring the

Right: **TE 1077 (LK60 AEY) was transferred from Cricklewood to Holloway in April 2015, following the receipt of a TEH. At the same time the 91's contract was awarded to and retained by Metroline for a further five years, with Borismasters scheduled to take over from February 2016. On 9 August 2015, this bus is seen at the Nag's Head, Holloway.** *Matthew Wharmby*

survival, albeit in a very small way, of London registrations on London buses!). They remained in store until it was decided where to deploy them; Metroline's frustrating habit of denying routes their contract-specified new buses by concentrating everything new on central London routes, in this case the 16, looked likely to continue until a change of mind ordered them allocated to the 332 as intended; after all, this route did share most of its roads with the 16. Despite continuing hold-ups, finally one entered service on 16 April; this was TEH 2082 as W56. Their entry into service allowed several 60-reg TEs to leave for Holloway, where the plan was for TP replacement but which in reality was converted to a scheme to displace VPs instead to take up a contract covering the Victoria Line closure during August. The last two MMC TEHs into Cricklewood thus entered service in the first week of June, and stuck firmly to the 332 other than very rare reported forays to the 16.

In June Cricklewood's TEH 1224 received a set of blind boxes of a material not unlike the readable paper used by Kindles; it was designed to give the appearance of proper blinds and looked very much like them. Fellow route-16 regular TEH 915 became the first Metroline hybrid to undergo refurbishment, and in doing so, lost not only Green Bus advertising livery, but the green

This page: **In spite of the fact that DDA regulations have ruined the ability of buses to display more than the absolute minimum of information on their blinds, the traditional linen (or Tyvek these days) remain expensive and inhibit flexibility. TfL, however, have been notably skittish in even thinking about using LEDs, as is universal now across the country, so a compromise was fitted to Cricklewood's TEH 1224 (LK61 BKD), using a pixellated base not unlike Amazon's Kindle e-reader. It could display the Johnston font with much greater effectiveness than could a set of LED blinds, but that was when it worked; the shot above of the vehicle at Oxford Circus on 9 November shows that a number panel has had to be stuck over the malfunctioning section so as to keep the bus available for service; below right is how it should look. Shown below is the rear view, captured on 26 September at Edgware Road. The side panel was different again, being a square box rather than the single-line rectangle normally carried, and experience saw that pack up even earlier than did the front number.** *All: Matthew Wharmby*

leaves from its original livery underneath. TE 670 regained red at the same time, ex-Invesco, and all five 'prototype' TEHs were done by October.

On 26 September Cricklewood's 16 was converted to LT operation, in order to displace its TEHs to start off the 168 (also at Cricklewood upon its takeover from Arriva London North) prior to its own conversion to Borismaster in 2016. A further LT conversion was announced in June in the form of the 91.

TE 1098 was restored to red in August after spending more than two years as a Lycamobile ad. At the end of September TE 1745 was returned from accident repair and entered service at Uxbridge.

Above: **TE 1096 (LK60 AHD) was transferred from Cricklewood to Potters Bar to take over the 307 from Arriva, and is seen on 19 December passing through Enfield.** *Matthew Wharmby*

Problems with the termini of both the 91 and 168 necessitated snap changes to the schedule for LT introduction on each, with knock-on effects to TE and TEH classes alike; it was envisaged that the 168 would now be done first and this commenced on 10 December, in good time to release enough TEs (and unused new Willesden VWHs) to Potters Bar to take over the 307 on the 12th. The tight clearance of the roundabout at

Right: **The 332's MMC TEHs are apt to wander; here at Waterloo on 25 January 2016 is TEH 2077 (LK15 CSU).** *Matthew Wharmby*

Crouch End where the 91 terminates was set to be addressed by getting rid of the roundabout altogether. In any case, the conversion was set for April 2016 with LTs 745-767 earmarked from the current tranche of deliveries, plus possibly short ST 2001.

In November TEH 1227 was treated to an ad for Green Bus. By January 2016, 'Kindle'-blinded TEH 1224 found itself on the 32, still having to have the number blind stuck on, but the experiment itself was otherwise declared a failure.

Above: **Just having passed its tenth birthday but still looking spry, helped by an intermediate repaint and refurbishment, is Holloway's TE 681 (LK55 KKP), seen at the last stop at Waterloo on 11 February 2016 before turning round to the north-facing stand. The 4 has been unlucky in that it hasn't had a complete allocation of brand new vehicles for over thirty years, since its OPO conversion on 2 February 1985; the TE itself is a strange visitor when 04-reg VPLs are otherwise specified.** *Matthew Wharmby*

Left: **Metroline's original blue-skirted livery is starting to become thin on the ground; here at the Angel on 15 July 2015 is Holloway's TE 924 (LK58 KGA) on a route otherwise operated by VW-class Volvo B9TLs.** *Matthew Wharmby*

Above: **At the time of going to press, the announcement was made of the plan to convert the 189 from TEH to Borismaster operation later in 2016; this had been rumoured for a while but was now reality. Here in Oxford Street on the morning of 16 January 2016 is Cricklewood's TEH 1229 (LK61 BKL).** *Matthew Wharmby*

Plans for 2016 involve the conversion of the E8 to 100% double-deck on 28 May, using the TEs displaced from the 91 by Borismasters. The 168 will then be converted to LT.

As of this year, the Enviro400 has now passed ten years in service with Metroline; 222 TEs are operated, plus 76 TEHs (of which sixteen are MMCs).

Registrations

TE 665-686	LK55 KJV/X-Z, KKA-H/J/L/M/O/P/R-V
TE 687-692	LK06 FLA, LK55 KKY/Z, KLA, LK06 FLB/C
TE 712-723	LK56 FHE-H/J/M/N-P/R-T
TE 724-738	LK07 AYZ, AZA-D/F-G/J/L/N/O/P/R/T/U
TE 828-847	LK57 AXF/G/H/J/M-P/R-Z, AYA-C
TE 878-888	LK08 DXO/P/R/S/U-Z, DYA
TE 889-914	LK08 NVD-H/J-M/N/P, LK58 CNE/F/N/O/U/V-Z, COA/H/J/U, CPE/F
TEH 915-919	SN08 AAO, LK58 CPN/O/U/V
TE 920-930	LK58 KFW-Z, KGA/E-G/J/N/O
TE 931-939	LK09 EKO, LK58 KGU/V/Y, LK09 EKP/R/T, LK58 KHC/D
TE 940-951	LK58 KHE-H, LK09 EKU, LK58 KHL/M/O/P/R/T/U
TE 976-992	LK59 DYY, DZA-H/J/L-P/R/S
TE 1073-1075	LK10 BZV/X/Y
TE 1076-1104	LK60 AEX/Y/Z, AFA/E/F/N/O/U/V/X-Z, AGO/U/V/Y/Z, AHA/C-E/G/J/L/N/O/P/U
TEH 1105-1114	LK60 AHV/X-Z, AJO/U/V/X/Y, AKF
TEH 1217-1242	LK61 BJO/U/V/X-Z, BKA/D-G/J/L/N/O/U/V/X-Z, BLF/J/N/V/X/Z, BMO
TE 1307-1317	LK12 AVD/J/N/T/U, AWA/C/J/N/O/P
TE 1420-1448	LK62 DXM/P/S/T/X/Y, DYA/C/D/F-H/N/O, LK13 BEU/Y, BFA/J/L-P/U/V/X-Z
TEH 1449-1467	LK13 BGE/F/O/U/V/X-Z, BHA/D-F/J/L/N/O/P/U/V
TEH 2072-2087	LK15 CWA/C, CRZ, CSF/O/U/V/X-Z, CTE/F, CUA/C-G/H

Date	Deliveries	Licensed for Service
12.05	TE 665-672	
01.06	TE 673-679	TE 665-679 (**HT**)
02.06	TE 680-686, 688-690	TE 680-686, 688-690 (**HT**)
03.06	TE 687, 691, 692	TE 687, 691, 692 (**HT**)
11.06	TE 712-723	TE 712-723 (**HT**)
03.07	TE 724, 725	TE 724, 725 (**EW**)
04.07	TE 726-738	TE 726-738 (**EW**)
10.07	TE 828-847	TE 828-842 (**W**), TE 843-847 (**EW**)
07.08	TE 878-886	TE 878-882 (**W**)
08.08	TE 889-902	TE 883-896, 898 (**W**)
09.08	TE 903-914	TE 897, 899-914 (**W**)
12.08	TEH 915-919	TEH 915-919 (**W**)
01.09	TE 920-926, 938, 939	
02.09	TE 927-936, 940-951	TE 920-930 (**HT**), TE 938-940, 942, 943, 946-951 (**PB**)
03.09	TE 937	TE 931-934 (**HT**), TE 935-937, 941, 944, 945 (**PB**)
08.09	TE 978-980	
09.09	TE 976, 977, 981-992	TE 976-992 (**AH**)
07.10	TE 1073-1075	
08.10		TE 1073-1075 (**W**)
10.10	TE 1076-1079	
11.10	TE 1080-1092, TEH 1105-1114	TE 1076-1085 (**W**)
12.10	TE 1093-1104	TE 1086-1104 (**W**)
01.11		TEH 1105-1114 (**W**)
10.11	TEH 1217-1224	TEH 1217-1224 (**W**)
12.11	TEH 1225-1242	TEH 1226, 1228, 1230, 1231 (**W**)
01.12		TEH 1225, 1227, 1229, 1232-1242 (**W**)
05.12	TE 1307-1317	
09.12		TE 1308, 1312, 1313, 1317 (**W**)
10.12		TE 1307, 1309-1311, 1315, 1316 (**W**)
11.12		TE 1314 (**W**)
02.13	TE 1420-1435	TE 1422-1424 (**PB**)
03.13	TE 1436-1448, TEH 1449-1457, 1460-1462	TE 1420, 1421, 1425-1433, 1436-1440 (**PB**)
04.13	TEH 1458, 1459, 1463-1467	TE 1441-1447 (**PB**), TE 1448, TEH 1453 (**W**)
05.13		TEH 1449-1452, 1456-1458, 1460-1466 (**W**)
06.13		TEH 1454, 1455, 1457, 1459, 1467 (**W**)
02.15	TEH 2072, 2074	
03.15	TEH 2073, 2075-2087	
04.15		TEH 2072-2074, 2076, 2077, 2079-2082 (**W**)
05.15		TEH 2075, 2078, 2084, 2086, 2087 (**W**)
06.15		TEH 2083, 2085 (**W**)

Acquired
22.06.13   TE 1571-1582, 1715-1751, 1981-2000 from First London

Arriva London

T 1-193, 201-284, HA 1-19

Curiously, of all the London operators of the Dennis Trident, Arriva (in its Arriva London North and South guises) completely snubbed the vehicle, only bulking out its tied DAF DB250RS(LF) purchases with Volvo B7TL chassis, but when the supply of the latter ran dry due to TfL dissatisfaction with its noise output, dabbled in the Trident's Enviro400 successor and discovered that it liked the model enough to become a volume purchaser, today operating over 270 of them.

At the end of 2007 VLW-operated Palmers Green 102 was retained and plans were laid to introduce new route 135 from Old Street to Crossharbour under the aegis of Barking garage. To this end, fifty new Enviro400s were ordered and soon increased to 65; the latter were proposed to furnish route 466, won back from Metrobus for autumn implementation. The class code chosen was plain T, the third such use in London of this letter.

T 1 arrived on 8 March 2008, after a late amendment to remove the black over the staircase panel, and was put into service on the 17th, not on the 102 at first but on school route 617. Service entry accompanied training, and by the end of March Ts had been seen on all of Palmers Green's routes 102, 125, 329, 617, 639 and 634. Blinds were carried for only this garage and not the otherwise accompanying Wood Green. Barking's had to enter service on 24 May with the introduction of the 135 so examples were put into this garage as a priority, just eleven having to suffice at Palmers Green; by this time they had all concentrated on the 102 as intended. Deliveries to Palmers Green then resumed, accounting for the first 47 Ts. Ts 48-66 were intended for the 466 at Croydon but due to early delivery, numbers from this batch would be run in first at Palmers Green, releasing DLAs to the training school to see off ageing Metrobuses. Barking's new buses soon took in visits to the 128, 173 and 275.

Left: **Ts 1-26 were the last to feature Arriva's yellow tape band; the 'cow horn' had long gone. Still in original condition when seen at Bishopsgate on 24 February 2014 is Barking's T 22 (LJ08 CUV).** *Matthew Wharmby*

Ts 51-57 arrived between 11-13 June and were soon deployed to Palmers Green, though on 18 July the first two were detached to Croydon to begin driver training. All were in stock by 24 August and two went into service on the 26th, one on the 60 and one on the 407. The 466 commenced on the 30th and even after that, sightings on the 50, 194, 197 and 412 were racked up quickly. Even the single-deck 312 was not immune. However, reliability problems on the 466 led to passenger complaints and the slow operation of the Ts' doors was blamed, so comparison trials were carried out with DWs over November and December before a new timetable was instigated that added a little more running time.

The phased run-down of the articulated bus across its London operators commenced in 2009, and the most controversial route to have been converted, the 38, was awarded back to Arriva London North with the promise of 70 new double-deckers. 57 new Wrightbus Gemini 2 DLs were ordered, and in February 18 an order was placed for 18 more Ts to join them.

Damage to Ts was already widespread; after two casualties had been repaired in 2008, T 29 was hit by a box van on the North Circular Road on 31 May and on 5 June T 63 was deroofed under Selsdon Road station bridge after failing to take the 412's diversion away from that structure.

The artics were on their way out, but Arriva didn't wait till 14 November before re-assigning the RM registrations on five of them to Ts 5, 17, 19, 24 and 30 to join a spare plate already allocated to T 7.

In September the 133 was won from London General after nineteen years and an order placed for 34 new Ts.

Ts 66-83 for the 38 at Clapton were completed in September and October and festured a new interior colour scheme for Arriva, with a grey floor, simpler turquoise seating moquette and ivory-coloured handrails. Together with the new DWs, they

took over the 38 on 14 November; also seeing Enviro400s at Clapton were routes 242, N38 and N242. T 86 was loaned to Norwood prior to Christmas so its drivers could train on the new vehicles in advance of the 23 January 2010 takeover date. Not all of them were available for service on the 133 and N133 by that date, due (as usual) to iBus fitment hold-ups, so VLAs from Norwood's existing allocation helped out, made spare by DLAs transferred temporarily. Wanderings were comparatively rare, but the 176 was an early adopter and the 2 was chosen specifically when buses were needed to cover the closure of the Victoria Line during 27 February.

The start of 2010 was positive for Arriva, bringing in the 341 from First and retaining the 168 and 349, while the 149 was slated for conversion from artic to double-deck; to begin with, 61 Ts were ordered. Across the river, there was also a new bus component for the tenders on routes 50, 198 and 250, and in the spring 15 further Ts were ordered to take in the 150, which would be coming from First later in the year.

It was decided to tackle the Arriva London South services first, Ts 118-144 being allocated to Thornton Heath for the 250 and Croydon for part of the 50.

Three more Enviro400s were given RM registrations taken off artics in June; they were Ts 85, 93 and 98 all from Norwood. T 7, however, lost its 7 CLT plate to a Caterham Super Seven; no disgrace there!

Left: **After the 133's batch came a contingent mostly for the 250 at Thornton Heath in replacement of the early DLAs, which were hardly superannuated by former standards but which were now cascaded away within the group. T 134 (LJ10 HUK) heads south through Brixton on 30 July 2011.**
Matthew Wharmby

The next T batch commenced delivery on 16 July and the first four were put to use as trainers at Lea Valley, Barking, Croydon and Thornton Heath, the four garages slated to get them. Ts 118-121 were allocated to Croydon, specifically to release six DLAs to Norwood, which would hand over an equivalent number of VLAs for a six-bus boost to the 159's PVR on 28 August. The four were officially for the 50 but when they entered service in August were mixed in with those already on the 466. Ts 122-144 were then deployed to Thornton Heath for the 250 (with appearances where appropriate on the 109 and 198). The building of the next buses on two concurrent lines, in order to expedite the production of those intended for the takeover of the 150 on 16 October, speeded up deliveries. Ts 180-193 were the buses allocated, and examples started as early as 5 October, taking in the 135, 173 and 275 before they were needed on the 150.

16 October was also the date for the takeup of the 341, with Ts 145-168 allocated to Lea Valley, and finally Ts 169-179 were for part of the 168 at Ash Grove, the first of these being sighted in service on the 26th. These released VLWs to Enfield for the 349, the other route due at least newer buses under its latest contract.

Below: **Arriva took Enviro400s in quantity enough to furnish three more routes at the end of 2010; one of them was the 150 at Barking, represented here at Ilford on 25 March 2012 by T 192 (LJ60 ATV).**
Matthew Wharmby

A whopping order for 78 Enviro400s was placed in April to fulfil the criteria for new buses on retained Arriva London North routes 144 and W3 (currently mostly VLW) at Wood Green and the 279 at Enfield (currently mostly DLA). They were promised from January 2012.

The first Arriva T to gain an all-over advertising livery was Norwood's T 102 in July, in blue for the M&Ms World store in Leicester Square (not, however, served by the bus's normal route 133). In October T 110 received an ad for the same concern but with a Christmas theme, and in November T 102's ad was amended to this version. December saw T 106 take a scheme plugging holidays in Calabria (southern Italy). The M&Ms buses reverted to red in February 2011 and T 102 in July.

On 15 October 2011 the W3 was transferred from Wood Green to Lea Valley where the 341's Ts could now appear on it. It was awaiting its own Ts in the New Year. A similar exercise began to wind down Beddington Farm garage, by which on 29 October the 403 was reallocated to Croydon and thus, in the fullness of time, became subject to T appearances.

At the end of 2011 the 78 new Enviro400s started arriving; or, to name them correctly following the rejigging of the chassis to accommodate ECWVTA requirements and a subtle refresh of the front light clusters and bumpers, E40Ds. Unfortunately, in the manner of the DWs of this type, fleetnumbers were skipped so that the new batch could start at T 201. Of these, Ts 201-223 were destined for Lea Valley's W3, Ts 224-259 for the 279 and N279 at Enfield and Ts 260-278 to Wood Green for the 144. They were built on two separate lines and were delivered out of sequence, though service entry to all three intended garages occurred in February, with the W3 commencing conversion on the 11th, the 279 on the 13th and the 144 on the 21st, though Wood Green's were just as likely to turn out on the 29 alongside DWs, plus the 141 and 221 less often. Enfield could soon be counted upon to spread its new buses to the 121, 307, 313, 317 and 349.

On 24 March 2012 the 34 was reallocated from Edmonton to Palmers Green, bringing

Above: **Conspicuously without any ownership details but arguably looking better that way at Waterloo on 18 April 2012 is Ash Grove's T 177 (LJ60 AUC).**
Matthew Wharmby

2011 would see the first Arriva T transfers. Despite having operated without difficulty alongside a majority of DWs, Ts 66-83 at Clapton were set to be replaced by further new DWs to the new European Community Whole Vehicle Type Approval specification and redeployed to Ash Grove to double-deck the 78 after thirteen years. This commenced in earnest on 16 April, but slow deliveries of the new DWs meant it could not be completed until June. Once blinds were printed with all of Ash Grove's routes on, the Ts began making appearances on the 254. Meanwhile, three Palmers Green Ts (45-47) were transferred to Croydon in April to alleviate shortages on the 194 and 197.

the possibility of Ts, but only through two weekday journeys and on Sundays as otherwise the route's DLAs would not fit so had to be parked at Lea Valley.

On the 31st Beddington Farm was closed operationally; the 264 was transferred to Croydon, bringing the chance of Ts. The 50 and 109 simultaneously lost this opportunity with their concentration at Brixton.

All-over ads were ramped up in the summer of 2012 to concide with the Olympics; Ts 98, 112, 113 and 191 were given a scheme for Vodafone in June and T 110 got one for the Samsung Galaxy S3. In July Ts 88 and 92 plugged Brazil (until August), Ts 53 and 57 Vodafone and Ts 189, 238 and 243 Visa (the latter two till September and T 189 till October). T 180 became another Vodafone ad in August. Samsung T 110 reverted to red in November but eight Ts (65-67, 94, 106, 107, 243 and 255) received schemes touting the Apple iPod; these lasted a month save for Ts 66, 67, 94 and 106, which made it into 2012.

From the summer the Sunday allocations on the 176 at Norwood and 349 at Enfield predominantly used Ts spare from the weekday PVR of the 133 and 279 respectively; very occasionally Norwood had put examples out on the 417. In October the 307 at Enfield was similarly modernised on Sundays. In July Palmers Green donated one T to Lea Valley and two to Ash Grove.

Arriva's preferred modern type was the DW class of Wrightbus Gemini 2, and those

Above right and right: **Lea Valley's complement of Ts for the W3 is represented on 27 May 2012 by T 202 (LJ61 CHF, *above right*) at Finsbury Park, while on the same day Wood Green's T 274 (LJ61 LHU) sets off from Finsbury Park.** *Both: Matthew Wharmby*

Above: **On 2 June 2013 Enfield's T 247 (LJ61 LKX) calls at Edmonton Police Station.**
Matthew Wharmby

into Wood Green from the very large order placed for 2013 delivery allowed the garage's nineteen Ts to transfer to Palmers Green for the 329 during March and April and release VLWs for sale; T 260 topped up Lea Valley.

On 27 April 2013 Ash Grove commenced operating the 106 as a win from Stagecoach East London; while DW-operated, a T was out on the first day!

What would prove to be the last order for Enviro400s as we knew them (prior to the development of the MMC body) was for Ts 279-287, nine E40Ds for the 60's retention at Croydon. Not needed till 31 August, they arrived in June and were put to use not only on the 60 but the 466. They were distinguishable by their white-on-black blinds, a new (or old) aesthetic feature recently introduced. In July

Right: **By the time the 60's top-up E40Ds arrived in 2013 white-on-black blinds had returned. On 6 January 2015 Croydon's T 281 (LJ13 CHO) crosses the roundabout in the town centre.** *Matthew Wharmby*

Ts 43 and 44 joined them from Ash Grove and T 42 ex-Lea Valley was added in August.

Refurbishments to the first 65 Ts were progressing during 2013, with those up to T 117 to follow straight after, while all Ts with ads were red again by mid-summer.

On 1 March 2014 Lea Valley had to be closed due to the site being requisitioned by its former owners, and to accompany the reactivation of Edmonton a raft of reallocations of routes and their buses was carried out. Where Ts were concerned, the 341 passed to Tottenham (allowing visits to the 76, 149 and 243) and the W3 returned to Wood Green (to which it reintroduced the T class only five months after the last straggler had departed!). The 34 was put wholly into Palmers Green, to which Ts 42 and 43 returned

Right: **The 198 at Thornton Heath has been DLA-operated on a permanent basis since 2003, but in the interests of flexibility has seen appearances from whatever the garage happened to have available at the time, so DWs and ultimately Ts have turned out where necessary. One such working is captured at West Croydon on 1 February 2015 in the shape of T 118 (LJ10 HVO), which has been fitted with the new white-on-black blinds.**
Matthew Wharmby

Right: **The 125 was lost to Metroline on 7 March 2015, but in the final weeks of Arriva London North's contract, Palmers Green had been putting out increasing numbers of Ts; for posterity, here is T 261 (LJ61 LJC) swinging into Southgate station's characteristic semi-circular forecourt on Sunday 18 January 2015.**
Matthew Wharmby

Right: **Slowly but surely, the original batch of Arriva London North Ts has been refurbished; you can tell by the new style of seat moquette, as on Palmers Green's T 43 (LJ08 CSV) arriving at Enfield on 27 February 2015. This is another to have been fitted with white-on-black blinds, though that does not necessarily accompany refurbishment.**
Matthew Wharmby

during July. Most of the garage's original batch of Ts had gone through refurbishment by the end of 2014, the work carried out by Hants & Dorset at Eastleigh; in the process two seats were lost from the lower deck.

Route 34 would trade one set of Enviro400s for another when on 8 November it was transferred on tender to Metroline, which worked it out of Potters Bar with its own TEs plus the intended VWH-class Volvo B5LHs. The second half of this batch of awards also sent the 125 the same way; it had been able to field Ts since they arrived at Palmers Green

and latterly was apt to do so exclusively on Sundays.

In February 2015 T 159 received an all-over ad for Invesco; it lasted till June.

Barking's route 135 was lost on 23 May, passing from Arriva London North to Go-Ahead, but its Ts were transferred to Thornton Heath to replace the last DLAs on the 198 and 250 (other than three extremely stubborn stragglers, which remain in service!). From August onwards Ts 12-26 began going through refurbishment as part of this new contract.

On 18 July T 59 was deroofed under Norwood Junction station bridge after taking the short cut to the 197's stand rather than the correct long way round.

The 78 now received its latest contract award, still with Arriva London North but with the promise of new buses. These were firmed up in the summer as yet another Enviro400 variant, the London-specific Enviro400City designed by Alexander Dennis with Borismaster cues so as to be in a good position to take the orders coming after the construction of all 800 production LTs. Mockups in *Buses* magazine of November 2015 showed the new asymmetric front adapted from the single-deck Enviro200 MMC, combined with a diagonal staircase window and a metal panel surrounding the blind boxes rather than tinted glass. 19 were ordered in time for a 14 November start, and would inaugurate a new HA class.

Existing Ts were also to move again; the 168 was lost to Metroline on 26 September, removing the likelihood of Arriva Enviro400s but introducing Metroline's own TEHs

from Holloway, pending the receipt of new Borismasters. The existing VLWs moved over to the 78 on a temporary basis pending its new Enviro400Citys, allowing its current Ts to transfer from Ash Grove to Barking and double-deck the 173 permanently. A refurbishment was part of this process, with buses beginning to go away during October. At the end of the month T 179 was re-registered WLT 719, taking the former Routemaster mark off departing DAF DW 19, but it reverted to its original mark before the end of 2015.

With a demonstrator in London red leading the way, the HAs began arriving at the end of November and the first entered service at Barking on 7 December. The interior was particularly smart, carying over the gold handrails and maroon sidewalls of the Borismaster and teaming it with a new maroon-based moquette also inspired by the LT class but with new roundel accents throughout.

The conversion of the 149 from DW to LT during October caused existing vehicle

Below: **The MMC City came as something of a surprise, being unveiled at Coach & Bus with an order already in production for Arriva London North. These transpired as HA 1-19 for the 78 out of Ash Grove, and the first examples entered service on 7 December. Nine days later, with the conversion from Ts (and, since the loss of the 135's examples, VLWs) ongoing, HA 5 (LK65 BZB) is captured at Peckham, with T 171 (LJ60 AUW) closed up behind.**
Matthew Wharmby

complements to start shifting; the displaced DB300s that didn't move to Enfield to put an end to VLWs and early DWs there stayed at Tottenham to take over the 341. This route's Ts began transferring to Norwood in December where their intended remit was to upgrade the 417 from 03-reg VLA to fulfil its retained tender terms. For the moment they began adding to the 133's fleet of only a year senior in age, and at the start of 2016 were turning out in strength on the 2. The HAs, meanwhile, started paying visits to the 106 during January, and even on the 254 once.

Longer-term plans for 2016 include the double-decking of the 368 upon its acquisition from Blue Triangle on 30 April; this will use Ts 169-179 displaced from the 78 at Ash Grove, after they have been put

Right: **Wanderings of Norwood Ts from their dedicated 133 to the 2 were rare until a large contingent arrived at the end of 2015 from Tottenham, theoretically for the 417 but in the event sticking to the 2. One of the indigenous ones is seen at Victoria on 25 January 2016 in the shape of T 116 (LJ59 LXS).** *Matthew Wharmby*

Below: **Since settling at Croydon following the closure of Beddington Farm, the 264 has undergone an official upgrade from the 'old' style of DW to the 'new', but the Ts new to the 60 persist in wandering; here setting off from Tooting Broadway on 23 February 2016 is T 283 (LJ13 CHX).** *Matthew Wharmby*

through refurbishment by Hants & Dorset. On a more strategic level, plans to increase the fleet as a whole are in train to officially incorporate the fleets of Arriva the Shires and Arriva Southern Counties, based at Garston and Dartford respectively. This will add 34 Enviro400s to stock and incorporate them into the T class; Ts 301-331 were already delivered as such to Dartford in January for the 229 and 492, while Arriva the Shires 5448 will be renumbered T 199 and Dartford's existing 6458-6470 will become Ts 288-300.

Registrations

T 1-65	LJ08 CVS-Z, CWA/C, CVF-H/K-P/R, CUU-Y, CVA-E, CTV-Z, CUA/C/G/H/K/O, CSO/U/V/X-Z, CYC/E-H/K/L/O/P/S, CXR-V
T 66-83	LJ59 ACY/Z, ADO/V/X/Z, AEA, ABF/K/N/O/U/V/X/Z, ACF/O, AAE
T 84-117	LJ59 LZD-H/K-O, LYT-Z, LZA-C, LYA/C/D/F-H/K/O/P/S, LXP/R-T
T 118-144	LJ10 HVO/P/R, HVA-H/K/L, HTZ, HUA/H/K/O/P/U/V/Y/Z, HTT-X
T 145-193	LJ60 AVR/T-Z, AWA/C, AVC-G/K/M-P, AUO/P/R/T-Y, AVB, ATZ, AUA/C/E/F/H/K-N, ASX/Z, ATF/K/N/O/U/V/X
T 201-278	LJ61 CHD/F-H/K/L/N/O/V/X, CGF/K/O/U/V/X-Z, CHC, CFM-O, CFP/U/V/X-Z, CGE, LLC-G/K/M-P, LKM-P/U/V/X-Z, LLA, LJY/Z, LJC/E/F/K/L/N/O/U/V/X, LHP/R/T-Y
T 279-287	LJ13 CHL/N/O/V/X/Y, CGG/K/O
HA 1-19	LK65 BYX-Z, BZA-G, BYM-P/R-V

Date	Deliveries	Licensed for Service
03.08	T 1-13, 15-20, 22	T 1-5, 7, 9, 10 (**AD**)
04.08	T 14, 21, 23-26	T 6, 8, 11 (**AD**), T 14, 21, 23-26 (**DX**)
05.08		T 12-25 (**DX**)
06.08	T 27-39, 51-57	T 27-29, 31, 51-57 (**AD**)
07.08	T 40-43	T 30, 32-43 (**AD**)
08.08	T 44-50, 58-65	T 44-47 (**AD**), T 48-52, 58-65 (**TC**)
09.09	T 66-74, 76-81	
10.09	T 75, 82, 83	T 66-83 (**CT**)
12.09	T 85-90, 92, 93, 95, 100	
01.10	T 84, 91, 94, 96-99, 101-106, 108-111, 113	T 84-106, 108-111, 113 (**N**)
02.10	T 107, 112, 114-117	T 107, 112, 114-117 (**N**)
07.10	T 118, 119, 121, 133	
08.10	T 120, 122-132, 134-144	T 118-121 (**TC**), T 122-144 (**TH**)
09.10	T 145-161, 163, 164, 179-183, 185	
10.10	T 162, 165-178, 184, 186-193	T 145-168 (**LV**), T 169-179 (**AE**), T 180-193 (**DX**)
01.12	T 224-226, 228-230, 260-267	
02.12	T 201-223, 227, 231-259, 268-278	T 201-223 (**LV**), T 224-259 (**E**), T 260-278 (**WN**)
06.13	T 279-287	T 279-286 (**TC**)
07.13		T 287 (**TC**)
11.15	HA 1-7	HA 1-7 (**AE**)
12.15	HA 8-15, 17, 18	HA 8-15, 17, 18 (**AE**)
01.16	HA 16, 19	HA 16, 19 (**AE**)

Re-Registrations

10.08	T 7 from LJ08 CVY to 7 CLT		05.10	T 98 from LJ59 LYX to 398 CLT
06.09	T 5 from LJ08 CVW to 205 CLT		06.10	T 7 from 7 CLT to LJ08 CVY
06.09	T 17 from LJ08 CVN to 217 CLT		07.10	T 70 from LJ59 ADX to 70 CLT
06.09	T 19 from LJ08 CVP to 519 CLT		01.12	T 3 from LJ08 CVU to 3 CLT
06.09	T 24 from LJ08 CUX to 324 CLT		08.13	T 3 from 3 CLT to LJ08 CVU
06.09	T 30 from LJ08 CVE to 330 CLT		10.15	T 179 from LJ60 AUF to WLT 719
05.10	T 85 from LJ59 LZE to 185 CLT		12.15	T 179 from WLT 719 to LJ60 AUF
05.10	T 93 from LJ59 LZO to 593 CLT			

Other Enviro400s

The Enviro400 designation does not always mean an integral bus, as the body was available from the outset for use on other chassis. However, only three such ever entered service in the original format, London General's VE 1-3, three Volvo B9TLs delivered for the 85 out of Putney and put into service on 13 October 2008.

As for the 'Trident' chassis, London General chose again to be unusual by ordering fifty-four of them with the Optare Esteem bodywork taken over from East Lancs; these formed the DOE class and entered service over the cusp of 2008-09 for the 93, 151 and 213, with visits to the 80, 163 and 164 where no single-deckers (usually of the equivalent single-deck SOE class) were available.

Much later, the MMC proved quicker to garner interest on chassis other than the 'Trident'; Docklands Buses' EHV class of sixteen Volvo B5LHs were taken for the 135 in mid-2015, followed simultaneously by Stagecoach 13061-13081 of the same combination for the 177 at Plumstead. At the start of 2016, Selkent added 21 more (13082-13102) for the 47 at Catford.

Below: **Seen setting off from Putney Bridge Station during the afternoon of 14 July 2014 is Putney's VE 1 (LX58 CWK).**
Matthew Wharmby

Left: **When on Volvo B5LH chassis, the Enviro400 MMC body takes on a squat and dumpy appearance, with a short wheelbase and long rear overhang, though within more or less the same dimensions as the Enviro400 chassis. Allocated to Docklands Buses' Silvertown depot for the 135 since 23 May 2015, EHV 16 (BL15 HBN) pulls up to Aldgate on 10 September.** *Matthew Wharmby*

Left: **Stagecoach Selkent have also gone for the MMC on Volvo B5LH chassis, following on numerically from a large Wright-bodied batch taken in 2014. Also allocated to Plumstead but meant for the 177, here at Woolwich on 10 September 2015 is 13067 (BF15 KGY).** *Matthew Wharmby*

Left: **Still a 'Trident', according to the manufacturer's plate carried within the entrance doorway, London General's DOE 6 (LX58 CWU) doesn't quite qualify as an Enviro400, as it has an Optare Olympus body. There were 54 of these, taken for Sutton's routes in 2009, and this one is pictured passing Kingston station on the morning of 27 May 2015.** *Matthew Wharmby*

Totals

Company	Diesel	Hybrid	MMC	MMC Hybrid	City Hybrid	Total
Go-Ahead	283	38				**321**
Abellio	158	86		47		**291**
Arriva Kent Thameside	43					**43**
Arriva the Shires	1					**1**
London United	73	51				**124**
Epsom Buses	18					**18**
CT Plus		1				**1**
Stagecoach London	277	129	7			**413**
First London	188	22				**210**
Tower Transit	10			3*		**13**
Metroline	222	60	16			**298**
Arriva London	280			1	19	**300**
TOTAL	**1553**	**387**	**23**	**51**	**19**	**2033**

* *Virtual Electric*